Moving Out of My Own Way

Moving Out of My Own Way

Creating a Life Worth Living

A spiritual self-help book for you to ponder, reflect upon, and to move out of <u>your</u> own way.

Moving Out of My Own Way: Creating a Life Worth Living

Moving Out of My Own Way

Creating a Life Worth Living

Dr. Carole F. Hysmith

MOVING OUT OF MY OWN WAY
Creating A Life Worth Living
Published By The Hysmith Group
Hysmithgroup.com

Copyright © 2016 The Hysmith Group
ALL RIGHTS RESERVED

No part of this book may be reproduced, distributed or transmitted in any form by any means, graphics, electronics, or mechanical, including photocopy, recording, taping, or by any information storage or retrieval system, without permission in writing from the publisher, except in the case of reprints in the context of reviews, quotes, or references.

Printed in the United States of America

ISBN (ebook): 978-0-9973117-1-6

Special discounts are available on bulk quantity purchases by book clubs, associations and special interest groups. For details email: dr.carole@hysmithgroup.com or call 770-682-1620.

A portion of all proceeds will go to
Victory for the World Church
Stone Mountain, Georgia 30083

ISBN (paperback): 978-0-9973117-0-9

To my

unknown ancestors, grandparents, parents,

siblings, husband, and

two children,

All of whom I love unconditionally!

Without them, I wouldn't be me.

Acknowledgement

Trust in the Lord with all your heart. Never rely on what you think you know. Remember the Lord in everything you do and he will show you the right way."
Proverbs 3:5-6

It took me almost three years to write this book. My first thought of whom to acknowledge in this passionate effort immediately turned to the Throne of Grace where our Almighty God sits. As I pondered on what and how much to share with you, I thank God for consistently leading me, guiding me, and filling me with His Holy Spirit.

Thank you, Mr. Hysmith, for being patient with me. I know there were times when you ardently needed me, but I had no emotional energy to meet that time of need. I am aware that sometimes I placed my needs as your wife and friend before yours. Nonetheless, I am forever grateful for your steady understanding, unwavering support, and unconditional love.

Thank you, Myishia and J.R, for trusting me to share intimate parts of your life with the reader. As your mother, I am grateful for your intelligence, personalized courage and deeply centered decision to help others by allowing me to share your life challenges.

I am forever indebted to my siblings, Malvane, Roberta, and Olivia, who helped me to revisit, reflect, and recall our childhood by sharing their individual perspectives on our past.

Without their help, support, and endorsement to *move out of my own way* and take the risk to reveal family secrets, this book would not have been published.

Thank you, Dr. Bessie Blake, wife, mother, educator, author, sister in Christ, and long-standing friend of over forty years, for mentoring me. You influenced me to see the importance of encouraging others to move out of their own way by candidly sharing my own victorious journey rather than through psychological theory.

Thank you, Lynn Prime, for being my loyal friend and supporter. You were there for me when I needed an ear and spiritual care and sustenance. I will be forever grateful for your alliance, editing skills, and flexibility when I more than once chose to change direction.   Your consistent words of encouragement, sense of humor, and, of course, delicious cuisines during our editing sessions were much more than I ever expected. Your care and support will never be forgotten.

I am also fortunate to have a loving extended family of nieces, nephews, and close friends who not only provided me with emotional care, but also technical support as needed. It was comforting to know they were always close by!

Finally, I am grateful to my anointed Pastor, Dr. Kenneth L. Samuel. Every Sunday I receive from his profound and thought-provoking messages the spiritual and intellectual nourishment I need to face the week ahead with faith, love, and unequivocal optimism. His passionate sermons helped me on many occasion to *move out of my own way* to overcome unexpected emotional obstacles. Today, I consistently apply this spiritual sustenance by keeping my eyes on the notion that I am a child of God who loves me unconditionally. So, thank you, Dr. Samuel, for your friendship, leadership, confidence, courage, integrity, and ethics. I *know* I have become a better person because of you.

Forward

"I thank my God every time I remember you." Philippians 1:3

In this revealing book, Dr. Carole Hysmith has done what most of us never muster the courage to do. She has dared to speak her own truth. Truth is not always nice and neat because truth is the raw representation of reality. But truth always frees us and sets us on a course toward self-identity, self-development, and self-determination.

People who are free have great agency to free other people. In telling her own story with such audacious honesty, Dr. Hysmith has invited all of us to name and claim our own tempestuous journeys toward better selfhood. Dr. Hysmith has shown us that there are certain things about our life's journey that can only be said best by us.

But it does take courage. Thank you, Carole. Your courage reflected in this book is a source of encouragement for all of us who are challenged to speak what we know about ourselves – even when it hurts. And thank you for inviting us to find hope, even in those hurtful places.

Rev. Dr. Kenneth L. Samuel,
Pastor and Organizer
Victory for the World Church,
Stone Mountain, Georgia

Table of Contents

ACKNOWLEDGEMENT I
FORWARD IX
TABLE OF CONTENTS X

INTRODUCTION 1

**LESSON ONE: THE GENESIS OF MY
UNKNOWN FUTURE** 9
    MY GRANDFATHER 10
    MY GRANDMOTHER AND HER CHILDREN 12
    MY MOTHER 13
    MY MOTHER'S SIBLINGS 14
    MY FATHER 25
    FATHER AND SONS 33
    THE LONESOME SON 36
    THE DRUG EPIDEMIC 37
    MY BROTHER'S LAST NIGHT 38
    FAMILY LEGACY 47
    MY OFFSPRING 49
    THE STIGMA OF MENTAL ILLNESS 55
    MOVING OUT OF MY OWN WAY 57

**LESSON TWO: THE CIRCLE OF LOVE:
CREATING A LIFE WORTH LIVING** 61
    OUR VALUES SHAPE OUR BEHAVIOR 65
    LEARNING OUR VALUES 64
    DYSFUNCTION BEGINS AT HOME 66
    POSITIVE VALUES 69
    NEGATIVE VALUES 70

THE BIBLE IS FILLED WITH VALUES 72
THE UNION BETWEEN A MOTHER AND HER ....
    SAME-GENDER LOVING DAUGHTER 75
A MOTHER'S VIEW OF HER ONLY DAUGHTER 75
MY DAUGHTER'S SECRET 79
A DAUGHTER'S VIEW 83
HER TRUE FEELINGS 85
THE UNION BETWEEN A MOTHER AND HER ONLY SON 87
A MOTHER'S VIEW OF HER ONLY SON 88
THE SYMPTONS 95
HIS TRUE FEELINGS 95
HIS TRUE CHARACTER 96
A SON'S VIEW 102
THE FIRST INGREDIENT:
    AN INHERENT VULNERABILITY TO EMOTIONS 102
THE SECOND INGREDIENT:
    THE IMPACT OF AN INVALIDATING ENVIRONMENT 103
THE THIRD INGREDIENT: "TIME" 106
KNOWLEDGE IS POWER 106

LESSON THREE - SEEKING LOVE:
THE JOURNEY OF ANTICIPATION 113
THE MYSTERY OF LOVE 114
MY "FREE CHOICE" PREROGATIVE 115
THE VIOLATION OF THE PSYCHOLOGICAL CONTRACT 120
ON BECOMING A DIVORCE STATISTIC 121
THE LIFE OF A SINGLE MOTHER 122
CHOICE: WHAT MOTIVATED ME TO REMARRY? 124
FINDING MYSELF 126
FINDING MY SOULMATE 128
THE CANOEING INCIDENT ...
    OR WHAT THE FIRST YEAR OF MARRIAGE MUST BE LIKE 131
MY "COUGAR" STATUS 140

THE SACRAMENT OF MARRIAGE 143
NAVIGATING THR TUNNEL OF LOVE AND MARRIAGE 144
THE ENTRANCE 144
THE HALFWAY POINT 145
THE END OF THE TUNNEL 149
CHOICE: I MARRIED MY "SOUL MATE" AND RIGHTFULLY SO! 151

LESSON FOUR - THE USE OF MY MOST PRECIOUS GIFT: THE FREEDOM OF CHOICE...153
THE USE OF MY MOST PRECIOUS GIFT: THE FREEDOM OF CHOICE ... 153
THE IMPACT BIRTH ORDER HAD ON MY FREEDOM OF CHOICE 156
THE MIDDLE CHILD SYNDROME 156
THE ROOT OF MY ANGER 157
FEELING VALUED: MY INHERENT NEED TO BE LOVED. 160
TRAVELLING DOWN MEMORY LANE 161
CHOOSING TO BECOME UNSTUCK 164
OUR PSYCHOLOGICAL NEED FOR CONTROL 167
ON BECOMING MORE SELF-AWARE 169
LOOKING IN THE MIRROR OF TRUTH THROUGH A FABLE
    CALLED "THE WONDERFUL WIZARD OF OZ" 170
SELF-DISCLOSURE IS LIBERATING 173
BECOMING UNSTUCK 174
ON BECOMING CONFIDENT, COMPOSED, AND CONTENT 179
TURNING THE PAGE 180

LESSON FIVE - THE DENIAL FACTOR: THE PAINFUL PROCESS OF LOOKING WITHIN 183
TO THY OWN SELF BE TRUE 185
LEARNING TO BECOME A CONSCIOUS COMMUNICATOR 187
MY EMOTIONAL CHOICES 189
THE POWER OF INTROSPECTION 192

OPTION ONE 193
OPTION TWO 193
OPTION THREE 193

LESSON SIX - THE SPIRITUAL AWAKENING JOURNEY 197
MY FIRST SPIRITUAL AWAKENING 199
THE REAL WORLD OF WORK 201
MY SECOND SPIRITUAL AWAKENING:
    A CANCER SURVIVOR AT AGE THIRTY-FOUR 203
MY THIRD SPIRITUAL AWAKENING:
    EARNING MY MASTERS DEGREE 207
MY FOURTH SPIRITUAL AWAKENING:
    MY DOCTORAL DEGREE 208
MY FIRST GUARDIAN ANGEL: MY SURGEON 210
MY SECOND GUARDIAN ANGEL: PEGGY 212
MY THIRD GUARDIAN ANGEL: LINNETTE 216

LESSON SEVEN - KEEPING GOD FIRST: MAINTAINING A LIFE WORTH LIVING 217
AN UNWAVERING FAITH IN GOD 218
MY FAMILY'S RELOCATION CHRONOLOGY 223
OLIVIA AND ARTURO 228
MY MOTHER, MAYA 228
MY DAUGHTER, MYISHIA 232
MY NIECES, MARIE AND LILLIAN 233
MY BROTHER, MALVANE 234
ROLAND AND I 235
OLIVIA AND ARTURO: THEIR SECOND RELOCATION 241
MALVANE: HIS SECOND RELOCATION 242
MY SON, J.R. AND MADELINE 243
MYISHIA: HER SECOND RELOCATION 244

Roberta and Levertis	245
Elizabeth and Edward	245
Irma and Thomas	246
My Surrogate Family: Charlene and Anthony	247
The "Circle of Love" Family Day	248
My Self Worth Today	251
The Power of Now	252

Introduction

"Fear not, for I am with you; be not dismayed, for I am your God; I will strengthen you, I will help you. I will uphold you with my righteous right hand." Isaiah 41:10

This book on *"Moving Out of My Own Way: Creating a Life Worth Living"* is a philosophical voyage on the arduous road I travelled to claim my destiny. It is a truth-seeking message on what I sometimes took for granted: the concept of the "Freedom of Choice". Specifically, it is a lesson on love and how some of my choices in life actually created hurdles, attitudes, and setbacks that affected the love I sought, the love I received and the love I gave. As I reflect on my past, keep in mind that it was *always* love that interconnected with my humble existence. Once I moved out of my own way of anger, resentment and confusion, I began to feel free, liberated, whole, and a confident child of God. I am sharing the lessons I learned that helped me to *move out of my own way* because I wish the same for you.

One of my biggest obstacles in breaking through any daunting phases in my complex life has been my own thinking. I will share with you the experiences that have taken me to a higher level of understanding of who I am, why I made some of the choices that I have made, and my conscious and spiritual reactions to life's challenges. These experiences include my heightened level of self-awareness and esteem, my ability to make conscious choice, my personal relationship with God, and my strategic reaction to life's challenges.

How was I able to save my life to make it worth living? Similar to Moses and the two million Israelites in their four decade-long exodus from Egypt, between 1958 and 1998, I wandered around unchartered territory for forty years, trying to find the way to my "Promised Land". The unmapped and unchartered region I was destined to fearlessly navigate was New York City where I was born and raised. It was yet to be journeyed, trekked, probed, prodded, explored, appreciated, enjoyed, reveled in, and celebrated by me before my world spiritually changed. In November 1998, I was guided by God's Holy Spirit to finally experience my Promised Land in the form of Atlanta, Georgia, appropriately located in what is known in America as the "Bible Belt".

The "Bible Belt" is a casual term used to describe a region in the southeastern and south central region of the United States. Most of its residents attend regular places of worship where strict fundamentalist Christianity dominates life. They are considered socially conservative evangelical Protestants who play a strong role in society and politics. Since I am neither a politician nor a Christian fundamentalist, I pondered as to what God's plan was for me here in this unfamiliar territory. What is God's resolve for guiding me to this location? I was raised as a Christian and, as a child, attended catholic school as well as weekly church services for eight years. As an adult in New York, contrary to my childhood, I did not have a church home. On occasion, however, I randomly attended church services from time to time.

My reflective journey began by consciously, purposefully, and consistently praying for God's divine intervention. I asked Him to help me examine my behaviors of the flesh. I understood that God created me in the flesh and unselfishly bestowed upon me His son, Jesus Christ, to redeem me. Strangely enough, I began to value my life and consider it worthy enough to be salvaged. I therefore opened up my mind and heart and began to reflect, introspect, and analyze my life. After much discernment and prayer, I revamped and self-corrected behaviors and attitudes that got in my way to being God-centered and at peace. With God's help, I became more conscious in my consistent interaction with my family, friends, neighbors, community, and the world at large…regardless of our differences. I put aside complaints and focused on praises. It was a dramatic shift in thinking and behavior and it definitely changed my life.

Eighteen years later, now settled in this new land of Atlanta, I have a different frame of mind. I am now inspired to attend church every Sunday and often Wednesday night services, as well. Why this change of direction? How did this happen? The clear and true explanation can only be that prior to residing in my "Promised Land", I had yet to learn God's word. So that I can consider myself approved in God's eyes, I have devoted myself to deeply studying the bible and attending weekly study groups. Since then, my husband, Roland, and I have also become committed and active members of my church by leading Bible Study classes within our Marriage Ministry.

Why is this history important for you to know? Socrates said, "The unexamined life is not worth living." In order for me to continue to *move out of my own way*, I am compelled to tell the story of my examined life. This book is my journey of enlightenment.

As you continue to process the contents of this book, you will recognize that it is possible to self-correct and move out of your own way through reflection and positive self-talk, but only if the desire is there. Beginning today, it is my wish that you will first pray for God's divine intervention by asking Him to help you to examine your behaviors of the flesh. With God's help, you will find that your choices will become more conscious and you will be led to a place of peace and understanding that is truly divine. With practice and awareness, you can deter your complaints and focus on the praises. I believe this shift in thinking and behavior will change your life. As Mahatma Gandhi once said:

> Watch your thoughts; they become your words;
> Watch your words; they become your behavior;
> Watch your behavior; it becomes your actions;
> Watch your actions, they become your destiny.

Today, I earnestly trust that God directed both my husband and I to the "Bible Belt" region for a particular divine purpose. Contrary to my northern experience, my family and friends here in Georgia are devout Christians who diligently attend weekly church services. Roland and I have been members of our church for almost fifteen years and have grown spiritually from the thought-provoking messages eloquently delivered by our anointed pastor, Rev. Dr. Kenneth L. Samuel. I am sometimes amazed by the steadfast devotion and loyalty of his followers.

Perhaps by my sharing this journey of twists and turns, courage and trepidation, risks and wisdom, I will unhurriedly place God in the center of your being as He is today in mine. Hopefully, through this gradual transition, you too will learn how to: forgive yourself for allowing any unpleasant impact points in your life to immobilize you; overcome fear and trepidation of the unknown, the unfamiliar, and the untried by worrying less; love more by optimally living within each precious moment that God has granted you; reflect on your past with a desire to regroup and let go to *move out of your own way;* finally, actualize through faith whatever God's plans are for you.

Your challenge is to learn how to consciously create a life worth living. To do this, as mortal human beings, much inner work is required. If you are to remove negative thinking and enhance your positive thoughts, the desire must be there to change your life. If you are reading this book, you are either curious about me, my life, my choices, or simply longing to create a life worth living.

There are seven lessons I have learned from experiences in my life that I want to share with you. These impact points are spiritual, practical and contemplative in nature. Most of the information contained in this book is testimonial-based, grounded in insight, guided by personal and professional experiences, and occasionally referenced through my research on a particular subject. The most comprehensive method to introspect, embrace, and enjoy this book is to seize each lesson with an open mind. Each of the following lessons is independent from the next lesson so they can be read and reflected upon in any order:

Lesson 1: The Genesis of My Unknown Future
Lesson 2: The Circle of Love: Creating a Life Worth Living

Lesson 3: Seeking Love: The Journey of Anticipation
Lesson 4: The Denial Factor: The Painful Process of Looking Within
Lesson 5: The Use of My Most Precious Gift: The Freedom of Choice
Lesson 6: The Spiritual Awakening Journey
Lesson 7: Keeping God First: Maintaining a Life Worth Living

     As I continue to open up to you throughout these pages, note that I am on a humbling lifelong journey. My goal is to maintain a spiritual path in which to live the balance of my life with zeal and worth. In other words, I am creating a life worth living. I sincerely hope you will enjoy this book of truth, wisdom, and courage. I also hope you too will learn valuable lessons to spiritually create a worthy life.

> **Look at your life so far, and say,**
>
> **"Nice Start!...Now let's get on with it."**
>
> **Dr. Henry Cloud**

Lesson One

The Genesis of My Unknown Future

"So now faith, hope, and love abide, these three; but the greatest of these is love." 1 Corinthians 13:13

In order for me to encourage those of you, who like me, may be dealing with dysfunction in your family, it is vital that I speak about my family history. The four generations you are about to be introduced to are responsible for shaping the woman I am today. It begins with the generation of my grandparents, parents, transitions into my generation, and closes with an introduction to the generation of my children.

Ellis Island

At the turn of the twentieth century, New York was considered to be the melting pot of the United Sates, filled with people from all over the nation and the world. Ellis Island, in Upper New York Bay, was the gateway for over twelve million immigrants to the United States. It is known as the nation's busiest immigrant inspection station from 1892 until 1954. Just envision what the streets must have looked like during this migration period. Due to the recent invention of the Model T by Henry Ford, between 1918 and the end of the 1920s, there were more than a half a million new motor vehicles on the streets of New York, including Harlem. Yet there had been no new highway construction within the city. Cars were choking the city with traffic. Consequently, the streets of Harlem were chaotic, filled with crowds of people of all races and ethnicities, bountiful vendors, black cars, and many faces of desperation and despair.

In the early 1900s, the largest numbers of black immigrants were English-speaking Caribbean or West Indian natives. They chose to settle in the Northeast, mainly New York City. These West Indian immigrants were only 1.3 percent of the New York City population. Consequently, they faced intense racism. My grandfather, who we knew as "Poppy," was one of the many immigrants who chose to settle in the bowels of New York City. Ellis Island was his entrance into his new world.

My Grandfather

"So, whether you eat or drink, or whatever you do, all to the glory of God."
John 15:16

By the time my grandfather arrived in Ellis Island in 1919 from St. Vincent, the British West Indies, demographics were actually shifting. He had heard that New York City was highly regarded as an era of prosperity. His vision of "overflowing milk and honey" quickly dissipated when the reality of the hardships of the "melting pot" was experienced and accepted by him. My grandfather also quickly discovered that the streets were not "paved with gold" as he expected. Unemployment amongst urban workers remained, on average, under seven percent. However, a continued labor surplus was fueled not only by immigration, but also by Black migration from the rural south to the urban streets of New York City. This migration was also exacerbated by industrialization, which precipitated the displacement of both skilled and unskilled workers with machines instead of manual labor. The shift in work principles caused limited improvements in wages and working conditions. Unfortunately it also insured continued levels of high unemployment and job insecurity.

By 1923, the growth of the West Indian population surged as the group became almost thirteen percent of the city's total population. Many of these immigrants were young, unmarried men. Historians and researchers have also determined that many of these immigrants had literacy levels above American blacks and even some whites. In other words, they were quite intelligent with strong work ethics. Therefore, a substantial number of West Indian immigrants attended night school and pursued higher education while in America. My grandfather was one of these immigrants who were eager to work and pursued higher education. Ultimately, like many of his friends, even with a high school diploma or degree, he had no choice but to become an elevator operator in order to survive.

Unfortunately, many West Indian immigrants entered the service sector working as doormen, laborers, and porters. This level of despair altered my grandfather's confidence and the vision he had for himself and his family. This was the beginning of the dysfunction that permeated future family generations.

In summary, the 1920s was an era of contradictions for New York as a modern industrial city that misled many immigrants like my grandfather who were entering the "melting pot". Nonetheless, "Poppy" paved the way for my grandmother's arrival from St. Vincent by investigating and experiencing the culture, limited job opportunities, sub-housing, and other means for survival.

My Grandmother and Her Children

"For I have plans for you, declares the Lord, plans to prosper you and not to harm you, plans to give you hope and a future." Jeremiah 29:11

My mother, Maya, was born on December 4th, 1914 in St. Vincent and the Grenadines, then a colony under the British West Indies. She arrived in New York City through Ellis Island when she was only five years old. During her exciting and adventurous ocean voyage on the Maravel, the same ship her father set sail on a year earlier, she was a very happy five-year old. Her attractive mother, my grandmother, whom we learned to call "Ma", observed her excitement. Her two-year old cousin, Henry, her mother's brother's child, also accompanied them. They were all eager and motivated to travel through the vast seas of the Caribbean Ocean, up the Atlantic Ocean, to their vision of their "Promised Land", New York City.

Harlem is a large neighborhood in the northern section of the New York City borough of Manhattan. Since the 1920s, Harlem has been known as a major African-American residential, cultural and business center. Originally a Dutch village, formally organized in 1658, it is named after the city of Haarlem in the Netherlands.

Upon docking in the summer of 1919, similar to my grandfather, my grandmother's high expectation of this new world quickly disappeared. Instead of the "gold bricks" and "flowing milk and honey" of her dreams, the streets were crowded with people, vendors, and many black cars. To add to her dismay, the process at Ellis Island was demanding, humbling, and drawn-out. Moreover, once they settled in their new environment in Harlem, my grandmother and my mother faced unbelievable hardships while existing on the streets of New York City. According to a Caribbean historian, Winston James, a few women arrived and held occupations as teachers, doctors, lawyers, and craftsmen. However, most women often worked in the domestic field as maids and nannies. The thousands of other competitive immigrants, including my ancestors, simply did what they could to survive in this chaos of lost hopes and dreams.

My Mother

"And blessed is she who believed that there would be a fulfillment of what was spoken to her from the Lord." Luke 1:45

During her formative years in Harlem, my mother, Maya, lived within a strict and unyielding West Indian family culture. Nonetheless, Maya was born with a gift of creativity and was fortunate to grow up during the era of the 1920's where Central and West Harlem were the focus of the Harlem Renaissance. It was there that an outpouring of artistic work took place without precedent in the American black community. Throughout her teenage and young adult years, my mother became inspired by this artistic movement. She had a burning desire to become an actress, or at least a piano player and singer. Conversely, with job losses during the time of the Great Depression and the deindustrialization of New York City after World War II, rates of crime and poverty significantly increased.

Moreover, her family's daily lives were challenged with poverty, survival encounters, and adaptation of constant intercultural changes. Consequently, the strict rules and demands imposed by her mother to stay focused on surviving quelled my mother's artistic desires.

Because Maya was the oldest child of four children, born with a loving and obedient disposition, her life was not her own until she married at age twenty-four. Prior to that liberation, her life was filled with demands, commands, stresses, and curtailments. As I understand it, growing up, many of my mother's dreams and aspirations were curtailed because of my grandmother's austerity. Ma was unrelentingly strict and stern, as remembered by family members. Maya's ambitious dreams of becoming an actress were countered almost daily as it was perceived by her mother as disrespectful; her desire to play the piano and sing were also discouraged. My grandmother not only had a stubborn streak in her personality, and, while highly valued, she was simultaneously feared. Additionally, she was also perceived as controlling, potent, and self-centered.

My Mother's Siblings

Within a ten-year period, my young grandfather was a busy man as my grandmother gave birth to three more children: Harry was born one year after my mother's arrival in the United States. This would make him six years younger than Maya and the second birth order of siblings; Nelson was born two years later, making him eight years younger than my mother, positioning him as the third birth order appearance; Margaret unexpectedly entered the world two years later, making her ten years younger than her sister, Maya, and the fourth and last sibling to be a part of this sibling birth-order hierarchy. Since Maya was the oldest of the siblings, age six when Harry was born, age eight when Nelson was born, and age ten when Margaret was born, she became their second mother. She loved and nurtured each of them with dedication and passion.

The Second Birth Order: Harry

Harry was not only handsome, but had an infectious personality. My mother was very proud of him as he grew up to be a man who was courageous, hard-working, and likeable. After serving his country in the United States Army, he returned home, met and fell in love with a divorced woman who had a child of about five years old. He was about twenty-four years old at the time. Harry loved children, which certainly added to his barrel of attributes. Being the loveable and attractive man that he was, they dated for a while and ultimately married. After about two years together, the family was aware that he was unhappy with his marital status. Apparently there were some value clashes in their relationship that soon became known to others. This was obvious by his shift in personality from a gregarious and a happy-go-lucky kind of guy to a disposition that became quiet, reserved, and withdrawn. As I understand it, if his behavior was diagnosed today in the twenty-first century, it would have been detected as clinically depressed. Perhaps this was a bellwether to my son's future diagnosis which I will share with you later in these lessons.

Harry provided for his family as a butcher in a meat market in Harlem. One day while at work, the rumor says he was inadvertently locked in the freezer, which resulted in walking pneumonia. We still don't know today how this happened. Was his marital discontent so intense, that he was not concentrating on his actions at work? Was his depression so deep that he should not have been working at all? Or was it purely an industrial freak accident that can happen to anyone who is preoccupied but not necessarily depressed? Did he simply prepare to leave, walk into the freezer to do one last chore, and the door inadvertently closed behind him? Fortunately, he was eventually discovered, released from the freezer, and life moved on. In the following weeks, however, Harry developed a persistent cough, shortness of breath, ongoing fatigue, loss of appetite, a low-grade fever, and finally chest pains that worsened as time went on. Unfortunately, Harry, at age twenty-eight, lost his life due to this incident that caused walking pneumonia. He was the first of two of my mother's siblings to lose his life at a young age, which traumatically affected the entire family.

The Third Birth Order: Nelson

Maya's middle brother, Nelson, was loved, nurtured, and spoiled as though he was her own child. Unfortunately, this fostering experience only lasted for a few years as he too died at a young age.

Nelson was only four years old when he contracted diphtheria, a serious disease that affected many young children at that time. Diphtheria is a serious bacterial infection that spreads easily from one person to another unless one is protected through vaccines. Apparently, Nelson was not protected and became infected within a six-week period of either being exposed to someone who was infected or by touching or drinking from infected receptacles. According to research, children under five and people over sixty are particularly at risk of getting diphtheria.

Of course, when a child is ill, parents can usually immediately pick up on it as the child is no longer as active. Maya, age twelve at the time, together with my grandmother, were astute and aware that Nelson was not himself. First, their concerns were minor as Nelson began complaining of a sore throat. They thought he was getting a cold. The concerns heightened when he eventually became very hoarse and almost couldn't be heard. Subsequently, he began having difficulty breathing and also developed a fever along with chills. It was obvious he was not doing well. By the time he was diagnosed, it was discovered that his lymph nodes in his neck were swollen and a thick gray membrane covered his tonsils and throat. I can only imagine their emotional discomfort and psychological suffering when both my grandmother and mother heard the terminal news of Nelson's illness.

During the era of the early roaring twenties, diphtheria was known as the "Plague among Children". In 1921, the United States recorded 206,000 cases of diphtheria, resulting in 15,520 deaths. Diphtheria death rates for children under the age of five years old ranged from about twenty percent. Fortunately, since the introduction of effective immunization in the mid 1920's, diphtheria rates have today dropped dramatically in the United States and abroad. Again, because of the lack of progress in modern medicine at the time, I can only visualize how Nelson must have suffered during his brief illness. By the grace of God, he transitioned to a higher place where he will suffer no more.

This experience was devastating for my grandparents as it would be for any parent who loses a child, especially a four-year old toddler. The memories of his first day at home, his gurgles, smiles, first steps, and first words were still freshly imprinted in their memory banks. According to Maya, because of her sisterly and nurturing connection to Nelson, she too was in an enormous amount of emotional pain. At the time of Nelson's birth, she was a mature and self-sufficient twelve-year old. Her two other siblings, Harry and Margaret, ages two and six, were still very much dependent on her direction as their older sister.

While Nelson transitioned from a dependent infant to a happy baby, to a growing toddler, Maya was there, lovingly assisting in raising him as if he were her own. Although he was her brother, her pain and suffering was boundless. She definitely missed him as she always spoke of Nelson in such a loving way. Nonetheless, she had to eventually put on a courageous face and move out of her own way to appreciate her other two siblings, Harry and Margaret.

The Fourth Birth Order: Margaret

As mentioned earlier, Maya's baby sister, Margaret was two years old when Nelson died. While my grandparents were mourning the loss of their son, Maya resorted to helping out as best she could by juggling her life and taking care of Margaret's needs. This was very challenging because Aunt Margaret was not an easy child to manage.

By the time Aunt Margaret was ten years old, my mother was twenty, single, and still living at home. Due to the financial limitations in the household, Maya had to drop out of high school at an early age. During the evenings, she attended night school to fulfill her dream of earning her high school diploma. Additionally, Maya also kept busy between helping out at home and working during the day as a domestic. On weekends, Maya was also very involved in church as a Sunday school teacher. My mother thought life would get a little easier as Aunt Margaret matured, but her baby sister had no desire to share in household chores and responsibilities.

Over the years, Aunt Margaret observed how my grandmother treated my mother. She noticed that Maya experienced most of the hardships, burdens, and stresses of family life under her mother's watchful eye. Aunt Margaret perceived that it was a relationship filled with control and she wanted no part of it. She felt that if she were compliant, her young life would be burdensome like her sister's. Therefore, she became a "runner".

By the time Aunt Margaret was twelve, she rebelled by leaving home for three to four days at a time. Where she went, we don't know. However, she would return home, deal with the consequences, and then leave again. Contrary to my mother's compliant personality, Aunt Margaret grew up to be the rebellious one in the family who chose not to acquiesce to the family demands. Therefore, even before she reached puberty, she was labeled as "difficult to manage". She behaved like this until she became an adult and eventually married for the first time.

Aunt Margaret's Love Life

The way the family stories go, Aunt Margaret woke up one morning and found her first young husband lying next to her dead as a doorknob. They were both in their twenties. When she told the story, she appeared to be very cavalier about their relationship as well as his death. While there were rumors of a drug overdose, it was never confirmed how he actually died. I also never got the impression from Aunt Margaret that she was in love with him. I later discovered there was no love lost between them because of the "abuse" incident.

When Margaret was three months pregnant, it seems that her young husband kicked her in the stomach, which resulted in a miscarriage of their first child. Since her husband's death, there were many boyfriends who followed. Aunt Margaret was simply a free spirit who didn't let grass grow under her feet. She was always on the go. Although Aunt Margaret was a rebel as a young woman, she eventually became our nanny while we were growing up. She lived with us while we were young and dependent and took good care of us while my mother worked.

As we matured, we realized that when Aunt Margaret was good, "she was very, very good, but when she was bad, she was horrid." Aunt Margaret liked to "bend her elbow"…as she would phrase it. Having a drink now and then was how she did this. Although she was a great housekeeper and cook, when under the influence of alcohol, she kept the household alive with her stories, character, and jokes. Additionally, Aunt Margaret was always ready to fight a good fight. We learned more about our grandparents, parents, Harry, and Nelson from the stories she would tell us. She also introduced us to music and dances of the thirties and forties. Not only would she show us the unique dances of the "olden days", she would also tell us about the excitement that took place at different clubs. There was seldom a dull moment.

While we were in her care, she would sometimes take one of us to the liquor store with her. When I was chosen, I considered this to be adventurous. Whenever she went to visit her boyfriend at his job, she also would take one of us with her. It was during these excursions that I was introduced to midtown Manhattan. At lunchtime, I would be taken to a restaurant called the "Automat" where I would insert a coin in a machine, and, ingeniously, my choice of a sandwich or dessert would be in front of me. All I had to do was open the glass door and take it! This was fascinating, as I had never seen such magic. These are the fond memories of Aunt Margaret.

My belief is that we all have an "Aunt Margaret" in our family or an "Uncle Joe". Aunt Margaret had two personalities. One was the side that drank alcohol, cursed people out, incited fights, and caused family dissension; the other personality was the sober side, where she was very quiet, reserved, and a homebody. However, we knew when the spirited side was about to surface. She would not say anything, but would prepare herself for her two or three-week excursion by arranging her hair in a sexy style, daub her face with makeup, and dress herself with her best outfit. A few weeks later, she would return home and walk in the door as though she never left. Aunt Margaret was still a "runner".

Eventually, as a mature adult, she married again, moved about three miles from us, remained active in our lives by attending every wedding, most graduations, and sometimes funerals. She and my mother actually remained close as sisters until Aunt Margaret's death at age sixty-five in the mid-eighties. Still today, we often laugh about her humorous antics. Our favorite conversations evolve around the labels she assigned to certain family members and friends. My daughter, Myishia, was called "Gypsy", my brother, Malvane was "Handwringer", my husband Roland was "Smiley" and my niece, Elizabeth was called "Miss Prim". To my amazement, I was labeled The "Millionaires". She also gave names to people outside of our family. Ever since our teenage years, we had known the names of certain friends of Aunt Margaret's as "Lips" because of his protruding lips, and "Poor Lee" because he had a glass eye. A long-standing tenant of hers was labeled "Hi-Fi," because he recently bought a German-made state of the art Hi-Fi music system which he blasted day and night. Since this indoctrination, "Hi-Fi" enjoyed his new name. These names were what we assumed for decades were their given names. We didn't know until much later that they were actually, and artfully, created by our Aunt's wicked imagination.

Rite of Passage

"Children, obey your parents in everything, for this pleases the Lord." Col 3:20

As my mother surpassed age twenty-one, my grandmother's self-interest included not wanting to lose her submissive and compliant daughter to marriage; therefore, dating for my mother was also a challenge. Getting permission to date, as I understand it, was quite a feat. It is a wonder she eventually met, fell in love, and ultimately married my father. A relative told me that these unyielding difficulties began when my mother was about four years old, still in the Caribbean. The story says that my mother, at an early age of four, was responsible to meet her mother's controlling demands and was made to wash socks every night before going to bed.

Through God's good graces, Maya was saved from these parent-child demands by the intervention of my father's love. In early 1937, when my mother was twenty-three years old, she met my father for the third time at a club in Harlem called the "Savoy Ballroom". She had previously met him a couple of times during intercession in the busy halls of night school. They were intelligent, ambitious, and similar in their desire to pursue their high school diploma. However, their relationship didn't become serious until this magical night at the Savoy Ballroom. At the time, she did not realize she had found the man of her dreams.

Although my mother by nature was relatively quiet, reserved, and very soft-spoken, she caught the heart of this striking looking man, my father. Over the next year, their relationship blossomed into a serious matter. Fortunately, after much scrutiny, my grandmother finally approved my father and gave her daughter her "Rite of Passage." My parents eventually married a year later, on September 4th, 1938. This was when she transitioned from her mother's daughter to her husband's wife.

For the first time in my mother's life, she was away from her mother's scrutiny as they moved out of Harlem to Queens, New York. Through this union, within a ten-year period, they produced five children, two boys and three girls.

Uncomfortable Memories of My Grandmother's Home

If my memory serves me right, I was perhaps only three years old when I experienced my grandparents' home for the first time. Prior to that, I may have been brought to see my grandparents as a baby, but this is when my recollection begins. The adventure originated with the subway ride with my parents and siblings. We travelled from the suburbs of Queens to the metropolitan city of Harlem. We left behind the tree-lined streets and neatly rowed houses and entered into a world filled with high-rise buildings, crowded street cars, and a parade of people on the streets, including children. Once we arrived, there was even more anticipation and excitement in recognizing that we would be riding the subway again to go home.

It appears that my grandparents were the primary renters on the floor where they lived. They resided on the fourth floor in a walk-up apartment with many bedrooms, called a "railroad flat". This term "railroad" describes a layout that resembles a typical passenger train car frequented during the mid-twentieth century or earlier. During those uncertain times of invasive crime, poverty, and hopelessness, in order to sustain their existence, available rooms in the primary renter's railroad apartment were leased out by the week to tenants. Most of the tenants were acquaintances that simply needed a place to stay.

Consequently, from time to time, there was dysfunctional behavior exhibited in my grandparent's' household, primarily as a result of the abuse of alcohol. Being a young child, I was aware of my discomfort in that environment and was anxious to go home.

My reminiscence also includes later visits to my grandmother's house where the front room or parlor was constantly filled with people. I often remember some of these times as an adventurous experience yet overwhelming because of the number of strangers I encountered. I was passed around from one lap to another as rancid breath men asked questions like "What do you want to be when you grow up?" or "Where did you get that pretty dress?" or "What's your favorite toy?" During these times I vividly recall my grandmother's presence but don't have too many memories of my grandfather, "Poppy". Due to the number of people who were constantly stopping by when we visited, perhaps he was somewhere in the building…perhaps not. This expose' is my first cathartic experience of imagining how my mother may have lived as a child. This dysfunctional behavior later repeated itself as we grew up in our household.

My Father

"Trust in the Lord with all your heart. Never rely on what you think you know. Remember the Lord in everything you do and he will show you the right way." Proverbs 3: 5-6

My father, like my mother, was also born in 1914 and migrated to New York City from Natchitoches, Louisiana in 1921 at the young age of seven. I understand my father's mother, my grandmother, was considered to be one of the most beautiful women in the Cane River community, a suburb of Natchitoches. His father, my grandfather, was also known as a distinguished looking man who passionately pursued my grandmother until they ultimately married. Previously wedded and a widower, my grandfather had one son and was at least two decades older than his new wife. Nonetheless, from this union, they had two children, my father and his baby brother. Unfortunately, through childbirth complications with the second child, my grandmother died when my father was five and his older half-brother was about sixteen. My father now was motherless. I often wonder about the impact this loss must have had on a child of five years old.

During that era in the southern culture, when death of a parent of small children occurred, it was typical for the children to be raised by extended family members. Therefore, an aunt raised my father, and his newborn baby brother. I'm not sure what happened to my grandfather after my grandmother's sudden death. No one seems to have that leg of the story.

The Migration

While affectionate, intelligent, adventurous, and courageous, Daddy grew up to be private and reserved. He never shared with us much about his past life of being born and raised in Natchitoches, Louisiana. When my father made the decision to become unstuck from his painful upbringing in the south and migrated to the north with his adult cousin, I believe he made a conscious choice never to go back. Even though he still had a younger brother, the culture of segregation and Jim Crow laws during the 1920's must have been so humiliating and disrespectful for him that he had no desire to visit or talk about it. He also had no desire to take his children to any southern region of the United States. What I do recall him telling us was that it was not an easy life. I don't believe he ever expected any of his children to migrate to the South, the region of the United States that, as a young boy, he ran away from.

In migrating to New York City, my father moved in with his step-brother and sister-in-law in Queens, New York, hoping to experience a more satisfying life than he experienced in the "Old South". He stayed with them until he married my mother at age twenty-four.

The Separation

Struggling to wade through the ups and downs of promises for a better life, five pregnancies, and proverbial hardships of the times, the give and take of marriage eventually took its toll on their relationship. After ten years together, my parents ultimately separated and went their distinct ways.

In retrospect, I understand how difficult this period of struggle, confusion, and overall sadness must have been for both my mother and father. During this tough first year of their separation and unhinged period in her life, my mother had to feel stuck and unstable. She was now the single mother of five children, ages nine, seven, five, four, and an infant of six months. How did she move out of her own way to manage and raise five children? My father, a responsible and accountable man, how and why did my father make such a tough decision to leave his wife and five children, especially his newborn son? How did he *"move out of his own way"* to make such a choice to turn the page of life to experience an independent existence?

A Courageous and Compromising Choice

At age thirty-four, my father made the courageous and conscious choice to pursue his own destiny. In order to do this, he had to make a decision to separate from his family. Regrettably, by the time my youngest brother William was born, my father had moved out and on with his separate but secretive and non-traditional life. You see, my father was born gay or better known today as a "same-gender loving person." My father was a good man, just different by virtue of his sexual orientation. What courage it must have taken for him to make such a compromising choice.

During the formative years of my parent's relationship, there was demonstrated love and happiness. The combination between my mother's loving and reserved spirit, my father's gregarious and adventurous nature, together with the joy of young, dependent, children in their lives was quite a formula. When my father made this decision to risk living an independent life as a same-gender loving man, I was simply too young to understand adult dynamics. So when he physically left, his spirit was still with us. For as long as I can remember, he never said a harsh word about my mother and constantly professed his love and respect for her. Nonetheless, he courageously chose to take care of his emotional needs, compromising his love for her and their life together.

Through the years following their separation, he consistently took responsibility for his family and our financial and emotional needs. He was very much involved with our daily lives and the many challenges we faced as a family unit until his demise many decades later. The biggest challenge that I recall from my childhood was when we were homeless.

The Impact of Eviction

I was only seven months old when we moved from my parent's first apartment after marriage. As their children arrived, including me, a larger apartment was needed. Because I was still an infant, I considered this three-bedroom apartment in Queens, New York, the only home I knew. We occupied the first floor of a spacious three-story house, lived on a tree-lined street with friendly diverse neighbors, and played with many Italian and the few Black children in the community.

Unfortunately, when I was seven years old, about the same time my parents separated, we were evicted from the only home I knew. At that time in my young life, I did not realize that my mom and dad were actually separated. Through my young eyes, we lived the life of an intact family. After all, we were the first family on the block to own a television. At that time in my life, I thought we were rich. I also naively thought all Daddies came and went as they pleased.

As I understand it, the landlord needed our apartment for a relative who was migrating from the south. Considering the break-up between my parents was still fresh, this news had to be daunting. Consequently, when the prospective tenant was about to arrive, we had a few days to pack up and leave with nowhere to go.

    Knowing my mother's disposition, she probably had many sleepless nights during this experience that were filled with anxiety and worry. My father's blood pressure must have also been high as I was told of the difficulty my father encountered in finding an apartment for a family of seven in a timely manner. His search was actually in vain as no one would rent their home or apartment to a family with five children.

    During the next five months, my mother and her five children received shelter from different friends and acquaintances. We eventually rented one small room, not an apartment, in a rooming house located over a movie theatre. These were not good memories for any of us as we lived together in one room for a few months under unfriendly conditions. The other children who resided in this building were not very nice to us. These tight quarters also required each of us to use a shared bathroom and heat food on an electric hot plate.

    Since we had no television, my seven-year old recall focused on small but significant memories: we were constantly together as a family unit, talking and playing together every day; we played with and nurtured our new six-month old adorable baby brother; for the first time in my life, I was introduced to the taste of sweet Karo corn syrup generously poured over hot pancakes; it's interesting how my taste buds affected my memory of this poignant time in my young life. Perhaps the sweetness of the syrup compensated for the bitterness of life we were then experiencing.

More importantly, as I observed in amazement, my sister, Roberta, created an altar and prayed for us every single night. She would diligently and humbly get on her knees before the altar and talk out loud to God. Being two years older than me, at nine years of age, the impact of our eviction circumstances was much greater for her than for me.

Answered Prayers

I can only visualize how overwhelming these months of the unknown must have been for my mother. However, it must have been comforting to know that her five children were safe and under her wings every step of this unforgettable journey. After being rejected repeatedly by apartment owners due to the number of children involved, my father eventually managed to borrow enough money from his long-standing friend and manager to add to his meager savings for the down payment on our own home.

I vividly remember the day we moved into this large two-story house not far from our previous dwelling. It was a warm sunny day in June 1950. I skipped down the street with my brothers and sisters, still not understanding that on this day we were moving into our very own house. Upon entering and being told this huge house was our new home, I quietly went from room to room and explored them in awe. We had a large backyard, five peach trees, and shrubbery that were not only bountiful, but also colorful. So many memories were planted in this house. We had great times, happy and, of course, sad times. Nonetheless, each of us lived in this house until we were either married, or left because, as adults, it was time to act like adults. If only walls can talk!

Although separated and in a committed relationship, Daddy continued to financially support us until we were independently on our own. And, while physically separated from his children, my father remained an integral part of our lives for his entire life. He was a good man, father, partner, and employee. During the forty plus years that he was employed at his one and only New York City job, he worked his way up from stock boy to manager in a textile manufacturing company, quite an amazing feat for a black man in those times. He also remained in a committed relationship with his one and only partner until his transition in 1975. This said a lot about his moral compass, work ethics, and character that motivated him to seek and actualize his vision and ambitions.

The After-Life

My father loved culture and the arts. During his separation status, he continued to introduce each of us to theatre life such as the ballet, opera, and Broadway plays. We were also introduced to diverse cultures such as "China Town", "Greenwich Village", and "Little Italy", which taught us the importance of respecting differences. He similarly exposed us to the wonder of national parks and other exciting and audacious activities. These experiences certainly added to our value system of diverse perspectives. They taught us to appreciate life through the exposure of a broader and brighter lens of the world.

However, my recall of my mother is that she seldom accompanied my father during any of our cultural expeditions or excursions. This could have been because they were actually living apart and uncomfortable around each other. Or, perhaps, being the compassionate woman she was, she was aware of my father's need to solely dote on his children as an independent dad. Deep down, knowing the reason behind their break-up, she may have recognized his internal conflict and need to be in our lives. Nonetheless, they both managed to *"move out of their own way"* to collaborate as parents to provide their children with an environment of love and support. Whatever they decided in their private discussions, it worked. They both remained in our lives until their last days.

Throughout our formative years, we saw our father so often that we did not accept that our parents were actually separated until much later in life. We were so naïve of this fact and my father's sexual orientation that we even gave our parents a surprise party on their fifteenth anniversary! We invited their friends and relatives and they all came. They each were aware of our parent's separate living situation, as well as the circumstances surrounding it. However, everyone who was invited was gracious enough not to make us look like fools by highlighting this knowledge. Our goal was simply to surprise our parents with a celebration of their union.

Father and Sons

"All that the Father gives me will come to me, and the one who comes to me I will certainly not cast out." John 6:37
Colossians 3:20

My oldest brother, Malvane, and youngest brother, William, had different relationships with my father than my sisters and I. Malvane, the first-born, suffered through many difficult experiences with my father. He was distraught by the decision that our parents were to separate. This is a heavy burden for a young boy of eleven to process and bear. He has three younger sisters and a baby brother who is eight years his junior. In many instances, he abhorred this birth order position even though he was very protective of us. In retrospect, my father had unrealistic expectations of my brother. He expected Malvane to step up to the plate and be the male role model that my father could not regularly provide because of his absence.

Malvane did everything he could to live up to these expectations. These were very high standards of spoken as well as unspoken expectations. Inevitably, these expectations affected Malvane throughout his adult years. For many years, his harbored resentment towards our father was transferred in the direction of my older sister, Roberta. Malvane's world was what he would term as "perfect" until his bubble burst two years later by the invasion of my sister's birth.

Prior to her birth, he not only had doting parents who unconditionally loved him as the first born, but also had devoted grandparents, aunts, and uncles. When my sister, Roberta, came into the picture, she innocently earned the second birth order status and unconsciously shattered what Malvane knew as his "perfect world." His anger manifested itself into bouts of bitterness, rage, and animosity. The resentment escalated even higher when I was born two years later, followed fourteen months later by another girl, my sister Olivia.

Finally, after going through the process of inheriting three sisters, Malvane became a pessimistic and resentful young eight year old. By the time he gained a brother, his level of distrust in what tomorrow will bring was ingrained. He not only survived through the experience of witnessing the ongoing pregnancies of his mother, but also the suspense of not knowing the gender of each new birth until our mother arrived home with his new sibling in her arms. Yet, through all of this unpleasant suspense, emotional roller coaster, and high expectations from our father, Malvane protected us as best he could. All of his friends and enemies knew not to get involved with Malvane's sisters or they would have to answer to him. This threat proved to be true on many occasions.

Forgiveness is a Virtue

I recently asked my brother to measure his relationship with our now deceased father, using a scale from one to ten, one being low and ten being high. His response surprised me as he rated the relationship a high nine. Twenty years prior to my father's death in 1975, when Malvane was just thirty-five, he said he would have rated the relationship as low as a five. He wasn't very happy with his father's relationship with "Uncle Joe". Fortunately, over the years, we all grow, learn from our experiences, and hopefully *move out of our own way*. It is an ongoing process that requires a certain level of self-examination. Malvane felt that it was a liberating experience to not only forgive himself for some of his unnecessary and childish behavior towards the relationship between our father and

"Uncle Joe", but also to forgive my father for his decision to abandon him as a small child.

These revelations were a result of a three-month period when Malvene and Daddy worked tirelessly together and began to have intimate conversations while spending quality time renovating our family home. Finally, my father and brother eventually reestablished their relationship and grew to know each other as adults and ultimately became good friends.

The Lonesome Son

"Submitting to one another out of reverence for Christ"
Ephesians 5:21

My two brothers had different experiences. Daddy's same-gender loving relationship was very difficult for both of them to accept. Malvane and William were polar opposites. While Malvane was a gregarious and true leader with many friends, William was reserved, a follower, and a loner. Through their young adult years, they were both adversely, yet individually, affected in the development of their father-son bond.

My baby brother, William, also suffered his own father-son tumultuous relationship. He really did not know our father the way his siblings did simply because my father started a new life when he was born. He missed the pleasure of having a daddy as a role model in his young life. This void ultimately affected his entire life, as their relationship never evolved. We all did well in school, but financially, college was out of the question for the girls and my brother, Malvane. It seems that my father was now in a financial position to send one of us to college.

When William graduated from high school, college was now a realistic option. Due to his high IQ with a strong grade point average, he was accepted at the prestigious LaGuardia School of Aeronautics. We were all so proud of him and showered him with verbal love and support. This act of allegiance toward William may have been the only way my father knew to make up for his absence and lack of emotional support in William's life. Unfortunately, this atonement never came to pass.

During William's college years, one by one, each of us married and left home. Even my mother became employed and was seldom around. Eventually, we were all gone and William was left alone. We did not realize until years later the impact our absence and empty home had on William. Our precious home, once filled with many people, voices, laughter, music, and guests was now silent. Later in life, William told my older sister, Roberta, how lonely he was in that empty house. He would wake up in the morning to silence in this large two-story house. He heard every sound in his footsteps, water faucet, and walls. When he returned home from work, he again faced the same level of silence.

The Drug Epidemic

During this emotional void in his life, he eventually dealt with his loneliness and perhaps resentment toward his current existence by getting caught up in the drug epidemic of the sixties. Subsequently, he experienced many failures in life, including dropping out of college, not being able to hold a job, and finally being admitted into a rehabilitation center for drug addicts. This was hard on all of us, including my father. Prior to this occurrence, none of us were ever influenced to move in a vulnerable or dangerous direction as it relates to the law.

As the years went by, the gap between my father and William grew even wider. My father remorsefully still held himself responsible for William's loneliness, sadness, and ultimate demise. Unfortunately, time did not allow him to make amends with William, nor with himself. William was the youngest and on drugs; for that reason, my father openly regretted not spending more time with him prior to this addiction.

Today, approximately ninety percent of all homeless and runaway children are from fatherless homes, which is thirty-two times the average. According to the Center for Disease Control, eighty-five percent of all children who show behavior disorders come from fatherless homes, which is twenty times the average. One more statistic I discovered to be of interest: research conducted at Columbia University found that children living in two-parent households, having a poor relationship with their father, are sixty-eight percent more likely to smoke, drink, or use drugs compared to all teens in two-parent households. This "absentee daddy" experience is just one of many associated with the dysfunctions of families today, especially when their absence affects their sons. As the last born of my siblings, my baby brother, William, was lonely for his mother, father, brother, and sisters. My siblings and I were totally unaware of William's emotional needs!

My Brother's Last Night

"Blessed are those who morn, for they shall be comforted." Matthew 5:4

They say that people have a sixth sense when they know their days are numbered. One cold winter night in January 1982, William was killed as a result of two hit and run accidents. On that unforgettable snowy night of his death, perfectly sober, William, who never learned to drive, decided to walk across town to pay a monetary debt. Family members attempted to discourage him from leaving the comfort of home because of the inclement weather. It was not only cold, but snow was rapidly falling like a blizzard. For some unknown reason, the payment of this debt was very important to him. We all knew it was a pretty long walk to challenge on such a cold night. Nonetheless, William was focused and determined to put closure on an unpaid debt and entered into the night. On his way back home, while crossing a typically quiet street, he slipped on a clump of ice and fell. In his attempt to get up, two cars were racing; one speeding car hit him while a second fast-moving car ran over him. This was about 11 PM on a Tuesday night. Neither car stopped to see if he was dead or alive.

My brother, Malvane, lived not far from where the accident happened. An acquaintance who witnessed the hit and run mishap immediately notified Malvane. He responded immediately, made it to the hospital, and was able to be with William just before passing away while on the operating table.

Subsequently, at 3:50 A.M., I received the dreaded telephone call that many of us fear in the middle of the night. My brother was dead and was now with his true Father in heaven. He was only thirty-two years old, but God called him home. Malvane later told me that I fainted when I heard the news. Even today, I have no distinct memory of what actually happened when I received this horrible message that my baby brother was dead. It was a painful emotional loss that I will never forget. My agony was compounded by the heartbreak I felt for my mother who was three thousand miles away when learning about the loss of her last born child.

As William's sister and advocate, I wish I had done more to fill his void of loneliness. I just didn't take the time to know him better through adult-adult conversations. Up until his death, he was simply still my "baby" brother who I loved and treated as my "baby brother". I loved him and today believe I could have done more.

Do you have a lost soul in your family who needs help? Now, and not later, is the time to think about what you can do in order to be more supportive of your loved one while he is still with us on earth.

As you can see, *moving out of my own way* required me to step outside of myself and assess how I was shaped by my experiences as a daughter, sister, middle child, and mother.

The Confession

I remember the night my father decided to have a face to face dialogue with Roberta and I about his "secret life". He pre-arranged to meet with my older sister, Roberta, and me at my home. His purpose was to share with us his position on his same-gender loving sexual orientation and to hear ours.

Although we knew he lived with "Uncle Joe", no one ever talked about the relationship. While sharing his life events with us, both Roberta and I were surprised with the level of emotion experienced during this confession by my father. After all these years, he was still having inner turmoil regarding his need to honor and protect his children from anything that may hurt us…even secrets. With tears rolling down his cheeks, he said he knew he was gay for most of his life and simply wanted to have a candid adult-adult discussion with us about it. He said he did not want to lose our respect of him by not giving us the opportunity to express our adult feelings about it. I recall my response was, "Is that all you wanted to share with us? This is a relief. I thought you were going to tell us you were dying!" That night, my level of respect for my father was enhanced if that was possible. My father had the ability, insight, and discipline to move out of his own way, conjure up the courage to be transparent, and to risk a response he was not psychologically, mentally, or emotionally ready to hear. His goal was to maintain our unaltered respect of him not only as our father, but as a same-gender loving man. He met his goal during that significant hour in our lives.

The Current-Day Dilemma

In 2016, we are still faced with the moral challenge of accepting differences in family dynamics. Although we are still confronted by differences in race, ethnicity, and gender, we are further more blatantly challenged in the reality of same-gender loving persons. Many of us still counter the belief that its origin is a genetic occurrence. Unfortunately, our values, principles and beliefs get in our way. In other words, what we learned as children has much to do with how we behave as adults.

Studies today are challenging the tenets of the notion that being gay is a choice rather than a biological fact. Based on a recent study published in a well-known journal, *Psychological Medicine,* "800 gay participants shared notable patterns in two regions of the human genome – one on the X chromosome and one on chromosome 8." According to the article, "This is the first study of its kind to boast such a robust sample size and also to be published in a scientific peer review."

Today, more researchers and scientists continue to investigate how genetics are associated with homosexuality. Therefore, more and more same-gender loving people are "coming out" with courage, confidence, and comfort. I wonder what it must have been like back in my father's era when this type of exposure was not acceptable by society. Therefore, his decision to step into the world of the unacceptable during that staunch era in the thirties, forties, and fifties took an enormous amount of introspection, courage, and compromise.

So you see, my love for my father was so strong that I did not allow his sexual orientation to *get in my way* of accepting all of him. I loved him just the way he was. My father felt liberated after our discussion, as he no longer had anything to hide or perhaps to be ashamed. Until my father's demise, he was simply always "Daddy" who left a legacy of being a loving, responsible, and accountable father.

The Reward of Respect

Over the years, my mother suffered with her own misery of losing the only man she truly loved. Remarkably, her love transcended the shame and pain of the whispers and gossip that swirled around the news that her husband abandoned her for another man. On some occasions, we heard muffled sentiments from others regarding their relationship, but never heard anything disparaging from my mother. She never spoke about their separation in a negative way, nor did she ever say a harsh word about our father or his partner in our presence. She even treated "Uncle Joe" with the utmost respect. My mother's remarkable inner strength and character helped shape the woman I have become.

As a psychologist, I know my father made a very difficult and challenging choice. He chose to be true to himself, despite the risk of being ostracized by family and friends. He had the courage to shed the outer shell of falsehood from his life in order to alleviate his emotional pain. Eventually my father moved to Greenwich Village in lower Manhattan where avant-garde lifestyles, such that shared by my father and his partner, gravitated.

Each of his children's lives have been shaped by the choice my father made at age thirty-four, the height of his life, to be true to himself at the expense of many people whom he loved. Nonetheless, in the end, my father and Uncle Joe remained together as a loyal, but unmarried, couple until their deaths in 1975 and 1977, respectively. Uncle Joe, an Irish man, became an accepted part of our family. For over thirty years, my sisters and I gave him the utmost respect as my father's lifelong partner, securing a place in our lives that even our children understood.

In my professional experience in counseling couples of varying gender configurations, contrary to what many heterosexuals think, the same-gender person relationship is not simply about sex; rather it is about companionship, feeling valued, and creating a life together to the same extent as heterosexuals. A relationship is a relationship regardless of the gender.

Given present day society's difficulty accepting the Lesbian, Gay, Bisexual, Transvestite, and Queer (LGBTQ) community, I can only imagine the emotional and psychological pain both of my parents must have experienced during the forties, fifties, and the sixties. What I learned from this experience is the importance of living my own life without judgment. As a result of this real-life education, I make every effort to live by this scripture, "Do not Judge, so that you won't be judged." Matthew 7:1

Based on what I shared with you so far about my father's level of integrity, ethics, and loyalty to his family and his partner, he certainly had to struggle to move out of his own way. I respectfully accepted him as my father for his character, including his life choices, and ultimately learned the importance of unconditional love.

Today, I can maturely empathize with my father's courage and conscious choice of walking away from his entire family when he did. This was a hard decision! No one wants to, or should be forced to, live a life of hypocrisy. I imagine a life of hypocrisy akin to being buried alive. The struggle for survival must be unbearably difficult, painful, and often hopeless. I feel such peace in knowing that in a bias-oriented world, my father and his partner were able to coexist as a loving couple for more than thirty years as responsible members of society. I can honestly say that my father's remarkable inner strength and character also helped shape the woman I have become.

As a footnote, in the end, Uncle Joe showed his appreciation for our level of respect toward him by including Roberta and I in his Last Will and Testament and left us a "Reward of Respect" through quite an inheritance. "To God Be the Glory!"

The Family Lineage That Molded Me Into Whom I Have Become

"My grace is sufficient for you, for my power is made perfect in weakness."
2 Corinthians 12:9

Similar to my ancestors, I am now a wife, parent, and sibling. I have learned their values, beliefs, and principles from their lineage as well as through the gift of discernment, *some* mistakes, and many experiences. I then applied what I know to be a moral compass in my lifetime, but have also evaluated and rejected a few values from my past. I believe we need to do this type of evaluation from time to time as all values are not perceived as good.

Since each generation consciously, unconsciously, and subliminally passes these tenets down to their children, I too passed these family creeds down to my children so they could do the same with their offspring. After having a better understanding of my family lineage, I can honestly say they molded me into whom I am today.

Regrettably, based on how I was raised, I also lacked expressing words of endearments to my children until I learned its importance and *moved out of my own way*. Through formal education and the study of human behavior, I eventually realized the lasting impact affirmation, affection, and the art of feeling valued can have on one's psychological and emotional development and well-being. To the contrary, the absence of these expressions of verbal love also has a profound, but adverse impact on one's psychological and emotional self-worth. Unfortunately, I became victimized by this deficiency in my safety net called "home"!

Today, because of my erratic and sometimes precarious childhood experiences, people in my life who I love unconditionally, are consistently affirmed by me through positive words of affection.

Ownership of My Dysfunctional Behavior

"Love your neighbor as yourself. There is no commandment greater than these." Mark 12:31

As an adult, I discovered that much of my unconscious dysfunctional behavior was established due to many childhood experiences. This awareness did not surface for me until I was mature enough for me to explore it. It was then that I reflected on certain impact points in my life. Retrospectively, I have learned that the hardships my parents' faced revealed how much I took for granted. This lack of honor for their many life encounters prevented me from examining who I am until much later in life's journey. Through false starts and numerous setbacks, I subsequently began asking myself four thought-provoking questions:

1. Were my parents emotionally well equipped to philosophically and psychologically guide me?
2. Did they provide the role modeling required for me to enthusiastically grow up healthy?
3. Were there too many siblings in the household for me to appreciate my value in the family unit?
4. Did I have a secure and safety-filled home of love and support?

When I honestly reflected on these questions and associated the answers with my current behavior, whether functional or dysfunctional, I was on my way to appreciating this characteristic of self-awareness that *"Love is bigger than you are."* So, again I ask, did feeling or not feeling valued drive my behavior toward shaping who I have become? I today know and feel confident in saying that love permeates every aspect of my being. Therefore, my thinking and behavior included the many choices I was faced with when making heart-wrenching decisions that, in the end, affected my future and well-being.

In order for me to passionately love another human being, I must first learn to love myself. It is solely up to me to unfailingly measure my level of happiness, source of contentment, satisfaction or dissatisfaction, or whether I simply feel empty or drained of any emotion whatsoever. Once I complete this self-evaluation, no matter where my results fall, I must then seek an environment of trust, words of love and encouragement, and finally take action to *move out of my own way* to attain self-love and an environment that supports it! The choice is mine.

Our Family Legacy

During my childhood, as mentioned earlier, my father was seldom at home. Again, in my young mind, I thought that his sporadic visits were commonplace. Sometimes he was there and other times he was not! I did not realize that this was unusual behavior in other households. However, I and my siblings have such fond memories of this man who we each called "Daddy".

When my father did visit, we would all anticipate his coming with words like, "Daddy's coming!" When my father arrived, he was warm, affectionate, funny, and filled our home with an element of excitement and much laughter. Sometimes, he even spent the night and our fun time would transfer into another day. When no one was looking, he would sometimes hold me on his knee and tell me, "You know you are my favorite daughter." How I loved to hear those words! It wasn't until we were adults that we discovered that those same words he shared with me were individually shared with my two sisters. We had a good laugh over this element of surprise.

When Daddy stayed overnight, we were in for a treat. We would wake up to the smell of hot chocolate, homemade biscuits, crisp bacon, and home fried potatoes, laced with onions and black pepper. Just thinking about those melancholic mornings stimulates my memory of the good days of my childhood. I recall these days of my father's presence in our home as if it were yesterday. I can actually see in my mind's eye my dad stirring the pot of homemade hot chocolate with the silver wrappings from the chocolate lying on the kitchen table. I can also smell the aroma of this sumptuous breakfast as though I am there with my mom, dad, and siblings' this very moment.

I mentioned that my father was the affectionate one in my family. Contrary to my mother's soft-spoken demeanor, he was the talker with a booming voice and a hearty laugh. He was the one who would lift us up in the air, cuddle us, place us on his knee, tell jokes, dance with us, and yet firmly scold us as needed. When my dad was around, my mother was happy and content and so were their children. Yet, my father definitely is remembered as a disciplinarian who expected his children to be mannerly, respectful, and sensitive to the plight of others. This same gender-loving father was one of the greatest men I know. He was not perfect, but who is?

Our family legacy discussions also include our gentle mother. Dissimilar to my mother's harsh and stringent upbringing, she was kind and sweet, a true role model, who taught us to treat all people as we wanted to be treated. Although we observed or experienced sporadic incidents of substance abuse, sexual abuse, and relationship abuse in our younger years, we were not allowed to call people bad names like "stupid, dumb, or ugly". We were even scolded if we mocked another person who was less fortunate than we were either physically, mentally, or economically. Dissimilar to her lack of affirming expressions, she was very vocal on those standards.

Retrospectively, my mother, a quiet spirit, a kind and selfless woman, a doting mother, unconsciously learned her customs and traditions from her parents. She then instinctively passed them down to us. These lessons were manifested in my upbringing and by example I passed them down to my children. I then shaped them into whom they have become.

My Offspring

"Therefore since we are God's offspring, we should not think that the divine being is like gold or silver or stone – an image made by human design and skill." Acts 17:29

I have been blessed with the miracle of giving birth to two physically beautiful children whom I love unconditionally. I highlight their physical beauty because of what I see. When my children were born, I examined their physical attributes: their ten little fingers, ten little toes, and their hereditary features such as my eyes, their daddy's nose, their grandfather's lips, or their grandmother's unique chin, rather than what I couldn't see. Unfortunately, what I could not see was the emotional and psychological challenges my children inevitably would be faced with as they grew and developed in life. The phenomenon of both emotional and psychological challenges would likely be experienced at some point in their lives, as they were in mine.

I gave birth to my first child at age fifteen due to statutory rape. Nonetheless, I married at the young age of nineteen and remained in that relationship until I was thirty-eight. Therefore, my children witnessed many of my marital stressors. While they were growing up, I was busy nurturing them as my precious children; busy assisting in providing them with their security needs such as shelter and safety; busy satisfying their extrinsic needs such as food and clothing. I was busy ensuring they had the education and foundation needed to lead a worthy life. However, I neglected to focus on their self-esteem needs, as I was not savvy enough at the time to consciously know how to do this. Consequently, by not placing as much emphasis on their emotional or psychological needs, I was blindsided by their challenges as adults.

The Unexpected Journey

You see, I had to move out of my own way in the acceptance of my first born, who happens to be a same gender-loving daughter. I also had to acknowledge, adapt, and accept my mature son's unexpected life challengers, the stigma of a mental illness.

Our first home was on the third floor of an apartment building without an elevator. My children still today refer to it as the "Brown House". Prior to my marriage and our new living arrangement, Myishia always slept in the bed with me. In this new environment she now slept alone. It was a small apartment with two bedrooms and it included a bathroom and kitchen that was shared with another tenant. My husband, Gary, age twenty-one at the time, and I shared a bedroom with the bassinet for J.R., while Myishia slept in a bedroom beyond the kitchen. The two bedrooms were separated by a window, and while we had immediate access to each other at all times, I was always concerned for Myishia's safety and her feelings of alienation. Because of the layout of the apartment, for my young daughter to go to the bathroom at night, she had to pass through the kitchen and hallway alone. Although Myishia never complained, the opening and closing of doors in the middle of the night for a five-year old must have been frightening.

The major changes in Myishia's life during this period of time, including the move to a new place, her new sleeping arrangements, and having to share her mother with a stepfather, probably was very upsetting to her. It likely became more intense after her brother was born. I often wondered what impact this experience had on her emotional health.

I share this background information with you because of the tumultuous relationship my two children had with each other as they grew and developed. The five-year age difference, the sexual orientation stigma, and the latent mental health issues, ultimately affected both of them throughout their childhood and into their adult years. Perhaps, as a mother, I can share something meaningful from these impact points in my life as well as theirs.

During my first marriage, I was guilty of the common trait of accepting subservience as a given rather than standing up for my rights as a strong, intelligent, and caring wife, mother, sister, daughter, and friend. I simply was not self-aware. I truly exemplified disrespect for myself through my meekness, passivity, and acquiescent response to my nineteen-year marriage. Disrespecting me to this extent gave sanction to my husband and others to also overlook my intrinsic needs.

Although my father was gay, I didn't recognize or accept my daughter's same gender-loving identity as she developed as a child nor as a teenager. It was mainly because my thinking stood in my own way by not wanting to admit to her sexual orientation. I believe there were signs, but I chose to ignore them. As parents, we want the best for our children. Being statistically identified or categorized as a same-gender loving person, I was not emotionally prepared to take this on. My concerns and obstacles had more to do with my needs rather than her needs. According to a study in 2008 by Stephanie A. Brill and Rachel Pepper for the American Psychological Association, it stated:

> *"…a person's gender identity develops in early childhood and some young children may not identify with the gender assigned to them at birth."*

Myishia later told me that she knew she was gay since she was six. She did not have a word to define how she felt, but she knew she was different. Therefore, I was in denial until she was eighteen. While she was in college, Myishia interacted with friends or classmates who did not meet with my approval. My disapproval was primarily due to what I considered to be disrespectful behavior. Their drug-related attitudes simply appalled me. I could not understand how Myishia even gravitated to these friends as in my mind, her values were different or perhaps more refined than theirs. Perhaps I was in denial since my expectations of her were so much higher. This was the period in our lives where our journey of disagreement and discord began. I angrily accepted the realization that she was gay, but for years I subtly tried to change her style of dress, hairstyles, and the company she kept.

In actuality, I was suggesting that she step out of her true identity and transform into someone who would be more acceptable to family, society, and me. I wanted her to meet my needs and not her needs. The impact point for me in accepting her drug addiction was when I received a desperate call from her for help. Upon reaching her destination, I was astonished to find her in an abandoned tenement living as a squatter in fifth and disarray. My fiancé and I brought her home and after a few weeks of detoxification, she desperately requested that we help her to leave the City of New York. She said she had too many dark memories here and wanted to start a new life. We immediately made arrangements with my mother for Myishia to travel to Los Angeles to live with her. My recall is that my mother was excited to have the company of her granddaughter as the only family member who also lived on the West Coast was my sister, Olivia. Once Myishia arrived and settled in, this was a short-lived arrangement. Myishia found a new life, and was ready for her independence. She ultimately gravitated again to the world of drugs and ended up staying on the West Coast for more than twenty years.

  Over time, primarily due to the thousands of miles between us, my position toward Myishia's lifestyle gradually lessoned. During this period of separation, I also grew and matured. I earned my bachelor's degree in psychology. This knowledge of human behavior helped me to see life from a broader lens. Now divorced, I continued my education to earn a master's degree, followed by a doctorate degree, all in the discipline of "psychology". This higher education journey helped me to grow not only as a professional, but also as a woman, mother, and divorcee. I didn't completely approve of Myishia's lifestyle, but began to recognize her more as an adult as opposed to simply my daughter.

  During this chasm between my daughter and me, I eventually remarried and relocated from New York to Georgia. This acceptance of my daughter for who she is and she of me as her mother was a three-decade battle for both of us. I had to learn to move out of my own way. I will elaborate on this battle further in the next lesson.

The Rude Awakening

J.R. left home as a young man of twenty-one years old and has always been independent. He has always been a productive citizen of society as an army veteran, a husband and provider, a leader in his community, and a loyal employee whose last position continued for seventeen years. His only flaw seemed to be his emotions which resulted in relationships gone bad. He married a few times, but now after ten years in this relationship, was again in the midst of a divorce. There definitely was something wrong. He ultimately was diagnosed with bi-polar depression and Borderline Personality Disorder, commonly known as BPD.

The Stigma of Mental Illness

Mental illness is considered to be a disease that is not accepted in society with ease. Once I became educated about the diagnosis and prognosis, I then moved from shame to confusion, and finally to motivation. I had a passionate desire to protect my son and subsequently become an advocate for removing the stereotypes. Although bi-polar is a result of a chemical imbalance, it is inappropriately and negatively labeled by family, friends, and society at large as untreatable, terminal, and shameful. At one time, I was part of this group. I've participated in and also heard words like "shame" "fear", "sicko", and "dangerous". These stigmas, implicit or explicit, simply exacerbate the illness.

Through avid research of its root, life-impacting implications, and prognosis, I subsequently removed the confusion of the stigma. I learned to understand that my self-esteem as a parent was still intact and I needed to focus on helping my son. I did not want to lose my son to the unknown. I subsequently had to move out of my own way and learn lessons from the emotional cycle of denial, anger, bargaining, acceptance, and finally movement toward the pivotal feeling of unconditional love.

The Love Conflict

Five years ago, with nowhere to go, for the first time in his adult status, J.R. requested from Roland and I to move into our home. Prior to this request, he had recently attempted to take his own life. He and his wife were in the midst of a pending divorce and he was in need of a safe place to regroup. I do know my son's inherent desire to be independent. So, this had to be a hard request for him to ask for help. This was the first time since he left home in his early twenties that I was approached by him for any type of support.

His stepfather, my current husband, was initially receptive, but ultimately had to move out of his own way to support this request. Embracing my son into our home was a difficult decision for Roland. For the twenty-five years that we were married, he never had to share me with anyone, including my adult children, and he preferred it that way.

As time moved on, he was not too pleased with this arrangement. Although there were times when we generously offered our home to other family members during their relocation transition, this was the first time the unknown was ahead of us. We had no idea how long J.R. would need our help. We also had no idea what the outcome would be. This was a difficult compromise my husband was making, but he made it in support of me.

Today, my son who still lives with me and Roland, has been treated, continues to be treated, and is doing well. Although we as a family still face challenges, with God's help, it is a good feeling to know that I did not give up on my son. I did not deny myself the joy of knowing my son is safe, supported in his daily struggles, and alive. Because of my lack of regrets, I am at peace. I place our future in God's Divine hands to help me in my quest to continue to move out of my own way.

For me, simultaneously and unconditionally loving both Roland and J.R. was a strain. Both of them subtly cried out for my attention. I knew, as Roland knew, that having two men in our home was going to be an ongoing conciliation and a challenge. However, my faith in God kept me spiritually sound. As long as J.R. was vulnerable and in need of my emotional support, with God's guidance, turning my back on him was not an option.

In the end, the strain lessoned for me in this "conflict of love". Roland eventually relaxed his position through prayer, his loyalty to me as his wife, and belief in the sacrament of marriage. In the end, getting past his emotions, he logically knew that this battle between a mother's love for her son and the love for her husband is a win-lose situation and one that should not be undertaken.

Moving Out of My Own Way

The benefit I received in researching my family's history was twofold:

1. I was able to psychologically step into their world to think about how they were shaped by their parent's generation.
2. This background gave me the antiquity I needed to reflect on my own dysfunctional, as well as functional, adult behavior as a wife, parent, sibling, and friend.

With the value of hindsight, it pleases me to know that my inborn and steadfast love for my children is even deeper in spite of the emotional and psychological challenges we all faced. Together, during our intimate journey as mother and children, we experienced the full circle of love by overcoming emotional scars in each of us. We have truly learned to move out of our own way. Today, as mature adults, we have become rich in accepting and appreciating the mutual growth in our abundantly advanced mother-child understandings.

What's important in this lesson on "The Genesis of My Unknown Future" is to emphasize the need to reflect on our past. Many of us have no idea or desire to know where we came from or who our ancestors are. As you can see, as it has done with me, this knowledge can strengthen you. I can now honestly have adult-to-adult discussions with my children or loved ones without shame or fear of reprisal. This dialogue will help them to sort through their lives as they encounter obstacles as adults that conflict with their values, beliefs, and principles. We all need to be affirmed to live our best life.

> *"Each generation has spiritual strengths and temptations that were shaped by the ideas and images of the times in which they grew up."*
>
> *Hayden Shaw*
>
> **Author of**
>
> "Generational IQ: Christianity Isn't Dying, Millennials Aren't the Problem, and the Future is Bright"

Lesson Two

The Circle of Love:
Creating a Life Worth Living

"Therefore, if anyone is in Christ, he is a new creation. The old has passed away; behold, the new has come." 2 Corinthians 5:17

It is so important to pause in life. It is this pause that helped me to reflect, document, and express my thoughts in an effort to move out of my own way from the busyness in my everyday life. Now that I know the history of my ancestors, this second lesson focuses on its significance. In this lesson I will share with you the impact reminiscing on my past and present generations had on the values that shaped my life. These values helped me to move out of my own way to honor the circle of love that is so important in creating a life worth living.

The Struggle to Survive

My father was influential in our lives, but it was my mother who instilled in us the value of the importance of family. She would say value-oriented phrases like "Blood is thicker than water!" or "Money doesn't grow on trees!", and would scold us if we complained about lack of money or we didn't look out for each other. We were together most of the time by eating, playing, and watching television together as an intact family. I can still recall the many days of fun and adventurous times I had with my four siblings.

As a typical homemaker of the day, my mother was also a gifted seamstress. My father worked the same textile company since he was fourteen years old. He would sometimes send home reams of material that was given to him by his manager and family friend. Subsequently, my mother proudly kept her three girls donned in beautifully hand-made look-alike dresses. Once in a while, she would make a dress for herself out of the same material she used for us girls. We would then be proudly displayed in our frilly uniformed appearance to close friends in our community.

My mother was a proud woman who would not, under any circumstances, accept charity. She would say, "As long as you have a brain between your two ears, you don't need charity." In other words, we are to work in order to have a relatively decent life. This standard was part of her West Indian culture and was consistently passed down to us. My father with his southern roots also expected us to live up to this same standard. We were taught how to survive rather than to attain wealth, become successful, or marry into a social class that would provide the comforts of a sophisticated life. We learned from both of our parents the meaning of humility.

Nonetheless, although my mother would not accept charity, she was not too proud to market her wares. If she had extra material, in order to make her budget stretch, she sometimes sold textile to her friends in the community and made arrangements for customized outfits. As a single mother of five, facing many financial, psychological, as well as emotional challenging trials and tribulations, she learned to move out of her own way by focusing on her children.

Growing up, I don't recall seeing a bible in our house. Spiritually, however, my mother taught us that "God is love" and that He loves all people unconditionally. Therefore, as a subset of our values, "Do unto others as they will do unto us", we seldom heard harsh words of cruelty, cursing, vindictiveness, or sentiments of prejudice in our home life. Interestingly enough, I guess because she did not use the bible to guide her, but rather used her personal relationship with God, we did not learn to judge others based on differences as depicted in the bible between Jews and gentiles.

Perhaps because of my father's southern roots, he was the one who researched and insisted that each of us attend a parochial school for eight years. Even though there was not a bible in our home, from this parochial experience, we did learn about the love of God and His commandments. Today, I realize that our spiritual foundation began and was nurtured during these formative years. Consequently, all five of us graduated from Our Lady of Sorrows Catholic School in Corona, Queens, which is a suburb in New York.

Our Values Shape Our Behavior

When I think of values, I define them as standards of behavior, attitudes, and beliefs that were passed down from generation to generation and are lived out at an unconscious level. In other words, as adults, we don't think about these values as we apply them. Most of the values we learned as children primarily came from family, sometimes subliminally, but also from school, church, and our community. Some were explicitly passed down to us through stories, words, actions, consequences and rewards. Others were implicitly learned from our experiences with parents, grandparents, school systems, churches, communities, and in some instances, our friends. The explicit or dominant values were consciously instilled in us by learning phrases such as "Thank you", "You are welcome", "No, Ma'am" or "Yes, Sir". We also had to place what my parents called a "handle" on an adult's name such as "Miss, Mrs., or Mr., Aunt, or Uncle". We received messages on the importance of respecting people in authority like our elders, teachers or managers. We also learned that the price of hard work correlates with a branding called "credibility" which can lead to independence and success. This journey of reflection helped me to appreciate my family and the circle of love we created. As you may suspect, these values did not easily come to pass.

Learning Our Values

We were taught by both of our parents to hold our own. However, it is primarily because of my mother that we are all independent today. I can still hear the words, "You made your bed, now lie in it." By virtue of my knowledge of my mother's upbringing in a non-American culture, I don't believe my grandparents had a bible in their household either. Reflectively, I don't believe my mother experienced the value of seeing and hearing loving words in scripture, at least not at home. My sense is that she never witnessed her mother on her knees in prayer. I also don't believe they followed the proverb, "A family that prays together, stays together."

As a child, I vaguely recall witnessing my mother humbling herself through prayer, but not often. I also don't have the recollection of the times my mother attended church with me, or my siblings. Therefore, today I have regrets about these experiences. In our household, in the absence of our father, we didn't hear scripture or "God loves you and so do I." I say this because, as children, we learn our primary values, good or bad, from our parents. My mother, nonetheless, raised her five children, even without the bible, to live a life of goodwill.

To my surprise, my mother did not openly express words of affirmation; it's probably because she never received it. We also never heard words of endearments like "sweetie", "honey", "baby", or other affectionate verbal expressions that may occur in other environments. We were seldom cuddled, hugged, or embraced as children, unless my father was visiting. The southern values he learned in his household were different; he demonstrated affection to each of us in our family without hesitation. He must have also known the bible as he referred to my oldest brother, Malvene, as "My son, Absalom!" We had no knowledge of what he was talking about, but to my dismay I later learned that, like my brother, Absalom was the estranged, yet beloved son, of King David. Similar to my brother, he was also described as the most handsome man in the kingdom, but out of all the king's children he was the most controversial.

My mother was a diminutive woman with a big heart. In stature, she was a woman of five foot three and never weighed more than one hundred ten pounds. Although small in size, she was a strong woman who overcame many obstacles in her current family life. During our childhood and adolescent years, in the absence of our father, we lived in a dysfunctional, yet family-oriented home. We were neither wealthy nor destitute. We were simply substantively provided for by both of my parents in meeting most of our family needs.

Dysfunction Begins at Home

Dysfunction has been in my family for as long as I can remember. I feel confident in stating that I'm not alone in this awareness since many families that I knew and still know today are considered dysfunctional. Many people have difficulty owning this label, but to *move out of my own way* I had to accept this reality. In principal, I like many other children of dysfunctional families, experienced unconscious destructive behavior while growing up. In other words, the unwarranted behavior I experienced was not intentional.

According to society norms, dysfunctional families are those families who can be described as single parent households, two-working parent households, and same-gender loving households. They may have no children, one child, or five to ten children. My father, the gregarious one in my parent's union, was also the sole monetary provider for his small and dependent five children. My mother didn't become employed until we were teenagers. Yet we were considered a dysfunctional family.

Dysfunction and Societal Norms

What dictate the dysfunction are societal norms that were contrary to the guidelines, beliefs, and philosophies initially introduced to the nucleus family. Some of these dysfunctions include substance abuse, spousal abuse, child abuse, and even animal abuse. I believe the root of this dysfunction is precipitated by the psychological need by a major figure in the family to impose dominance and control on those who appeared the weaker or subordinate family member. In most instances, the victim is a woman or child. One's self esteem is enhanced through power. This unconscious dysfunctional behavior sometimes causes other family members to sanction or value such behavior. Children then grow up in such families with the understanding that such behavior is considered normal. I certainly did.

John Bradshaw, a family-systems therapy advocate and family dynamics expert, captured his thoughts on Family Dysfunction through a familiar Internet site called "The Big Answer". Mr. Bradshaw's thoughtful clarifications on how dysfunctional behavior is linked to generational cultures reverberated for me to introspect and intensely think about my past. He reaffirmed my sentiments on the importance of entering or reentering family discussions regarding the generation who shaped us into whom we have become as adults:

"As 96 percent of families are to some degree emotionally impaired, the unhealthy rules we're living by are handed down from one Generation to another and ultimately to society at large. Our society is sick because our families are sick. And our families are sick because we are living by inherited rules we never wrote."

It's Not the Intent: It's the Impact

In my life, I was subjected to family conflict, alcohol abuse, sexual abuse, and more importantly but subtle, the lack of verbal affirmations and other subliminal messages of discouragement. I was not overtly discouraged or put down by my parents, but not necessarily encouraged or approved either. As part of my mother's personality, she was not one who ever put a person down through negative language or behavior. Most people, including me, considered her to be a kind and gentle spirit. However, she was not one who expressed her love for her children through such verbal sentiments as, "I love you sugarplum" or "Come here sweetie so I can give you a hug", or "You can be anything you want to be when you become an adult."

Consequently, as a child, I did not always feel valued. This lack of feeling valued or appreciated for who I am manifested itself later in life as an adult. I was, therefore, challenged with out-of-control anger episodes that could have escalated to unemployment, a jail sentence, or even death. From my personal and professional experiences, counseling engagements, as well as research, I have learned that we have more dysfunctional responses to our childhood experiences than not.

However, as I slowly moved through the maturation process toward adulthood, this lack of "expression of love" adversely affected my level of self-esteem or how I felt about myself. Apparently, many of us are born with this gene to be affirmed. I was no different. As stated earlier, I had an inherent and profound need to feel valued and loved. My mother simply lacked the voice to provide me, her middle child, with needed affirmations. I needed to receive "expressed love" by her, but this simply was not part of my mother's personality. Just as I was unaware of the impact this omission of affirming expressions will have on my life, so was she unaware. Although my father was in our lives, it was my mother who had the greatest impact on my overall childhood development, some positive and some negative.

Positive Values

On the implicit or unspoken side, my siblings and I observed or experienced both positive and negative values, beliefs and attitudes. What are positive values? Positive values include living in an organized household, consistently attending church, dining together as a family unit, observing holidays together, and witnessing parents who exhibit behaviors of accountability and responsibility through effort or hard work. Others include the importance of having God in our lives, family cohesiveness, love for our neighbors, applying hard work to live and progress in our lives, and to treat people as we want to be treated…with respect. These values are considered the ideals. However, we each grew up to have a unique perspective on how we view marriage and commitment, family relationships, loyalty, work ethics, religion and spirituality, sharing responsibility, time, decision making, money management, and discipline.

My father, who we called "Daddy", liked to travel. He was an experienced traveler who toured around the world and would share anecdotes with us regarding his adventures. I now realize that our implicit values and the stories we heard as children, motivated us to open up our thinking and to become adventurers and risk takers like him. These are just some examples of positive values exhibited in many families, including ours.

Negative Values

What are negative values? Everything that does not add to your well-being in a positive way are called "negative values". Unfortunately, as children, we also experienced subliminal negative messages that produced unsavory thoughts and behaviors. As adults, my siblings and I were able to candidly discuss these unpleasant occurrences. We now know, and acknowledge, that some of the incidences we observed were decidedly dysfunctional. They include frequent observations of alcohol infused weekend brawls, sexual abuse, spontaneous physical altercations, unwanted relatives as household guests, and unfamiliar men sporadically living with us. These negative messages are also called "values". These incidences became unconscious desires that we could have lived out in our adult years. Fortunately, as mature adults, we were able to use discernment in evaluating our childhood years, our positive values, our negative values, beliefs, and principles and their impact on our dreams, aspirations, and adult behavior. With this knowledge, we were eventually able to move *out of our own way* to create better lives. These are just a few of the standards of behavior we learned to apply in our everyday lives while growing up.

Terence T. Gorski, a prolific author and internationally recognized expert on emotional and mental health, in 1993 wrote:

"If you are among the millions of Americans struggling to get love right, the odds are you came from a dysfunctional family. In fact, in the United States today, more people come from dysfunctional families than healthy families. It is estimated that approximately 70 to 80 percent come from dysfunctional families. Consequently, being normal in the United States today has very little to do with being emotionally healthy."

This awareness can certainly be daunting for many of us. Therefore, Mr. Gorski went on to say:

"How can these figures be right? As we become more aware of how families work and how healthy behavior patterns are set, we recognize that child abuse, substance abuse, and other destructive behaviors affect far more people than we realized even a generation ago. By contrast, a functional family is one that teaches children how to think clearly and act responsibly, to understand their feelings, and relate to others in a healthy way. It equips them with the mental, emotional, and living skills required as an adult. To the extent that your family failed to teach these important skills, it was dysfunctional. Children raised in dysfunctional families develop a way of thinking about and viewing the world that is not shared by others. As a result, they have a hard time understanding people from functional families and vice versa. It is as if they come from different worlds."

A generation later, research by the US Census Bureau validated that the percentages of dysfunctional families are about the same today. Here is some data from 2008:

> *"The "traditional" family in which the husband is the breadwinner and the wife is a full-time homemaker has declined from sixty percent of all U.S. families in 1972 to twenty-nine percent in 2007.*
> *Almost 19 million American singles ages thirty to forty-four have never been married, representing thirty-one percent of all people in that age group.*
> *Today, the median age at first marriage is higher than at any time since 1890: twenty-seven and a half years for men and twenty-five and a half years for women.*
> *On average, first marriages that end in divorce last about eight years.*
> *The percentage of children under age eighteen living with two married parents fell from seventy-seven percent in 1980 to sixty-seven percent in 2008.*
> *Single-parent American households increased from 11 percent of all households in 1970 to 29 percent in 2007.*

So, as you can see from these statistics, our family values have shifted over the years to the point where the majority of us come from dysfunctional families. Hopefully, this awareness will help you to examine your family history and how it has shaped your life.

The Bible is Filled With Values

Today, living in the Bible belt, we are aligned with the values taught to us by our parents as well as the bible. Not only do we each have a bible in our respective households, many of us also know its contents. Contingent upon whom we are, how we were raised, and the church we attend, our response to God's word is different. My experience is that God's word in the bible can intuitively be misinterpreted causing us to adversely judge others. This diversity in our thinking and understanding of God's word can unduly result in feelings of alienation, devalue, and most importantly separation of God's people. Conversely, my experiences here in the Bible Belt are confusing. Three of the most significant superfluous biases that I've experienced across all races include: classism, racism, and homophobia.

    I am today grateful that as a child I didn't learn the bible in my home. If I had, I also might be the Christian who judges people according to my personalized, but perhaps altered scriptural-interpretation of God's Word. Through weekly church services, personal study, weekly fellowship, and healthy discussion as a mature adult, I learned about the "peace and joy" associated with knowing God's word. I was able to ask questions of clarification before accepting another's interpretation of their perceptions. I was able to look at the world from the eyes of Jesus, and respond to situations and circumstances according to His behavior when He walked the earth.

    My comments are not meant to offend anyone, but rather to highlight how the reflection on my past experiences, humble rearing, Catholic education, and values shaped how I view the world and who I have become today. I have been conditioned to live by the Catholic version of God's Ten Commandments which have never been burdensome:

1. I am the Lord your God; you shall not have strange gods before Me.
2. You shall not take the name of the Lord your God in vain.
3. Remember to keep holy the Lord's Day.
4. Honor your father and your mother.
5. You shall not kill.
6. You shall not commit adultery.
7. You shall not steal.
8. You shall not bear false witness against your neighbor.
9. You shall not covet your neighbor's wife.
10. You shall not covet your neighbor's goods.

Although I don't remember ever attending church with my mother, today I know she weathered the storm of her developmental years and grew up to become a strong-willed woman of spiritual substance. For this I am grateful.

Again, I give credit to my mother, along with my father, who helped to shape me into whom I am today. Despite the dysfunction in our family, my parents were good people and I loved them unconditionally. Because of them, and by studying God's word, I was able to create a life worth living.

In summary, appreciating my gift of discernment, attending Catholic school for eight years, and training myself to be present at weekly church services prepared me for my current life.

The Union between a Mother and Her Same-Gender Loving Daughter

"Train up a child in the way he should go; even when he is old he will not depart from it." Proverbs 22:6

My evaluation of true maternal love did not take place until I became a mother for the second time. Five years earlier, when my daughter was born, I simply didn't know how to verbally express love in a way that felt true and natural. Retrospectively, birthing a child at the young age of fifteen ultimately hurts both mother and child. Outside of the natural and maternal bond developed between my daughter and me, there was an emotional void between us that took years to overcome and heal.

A Mother's View of Her Only Daughter

"I have no greater joy than to hear that my children are walking in truth." John 1:14

My daughter, Myishia, my first-born, very early in her young life, expressed her love for me by innocently embracing me as her friend and confidant. Myishia can be described as a "free spirit" who got the short end of the stick because I was so young when she was born. As a young mother, age fifteen, and still in high school, I kept my secret of being pregnant for the full nine months. If anyone noticed I was gaining weight or becoming fuller, neither my mother nor siblings ever mentioned it. When it came time to deliver my daughter, everyone in my household was surprised. An ambulance was called and four hours later my daughter was born. One day I'm a young teen and the next day I became a mother. I was no longer a teenager, but a woman in a child's body.

    When my father came to visit me in the hospital after the birth of my child, he was beside himself with anger and hurt. During this intimate and difficult conversation, he reminded me that education was of grave importance to him and he was emphatic about giving my daughter up for adoption or placing her in a foster home so that I could finish high school. My mother worked full-time to help support us, so she did not have the luxury to offer help in raising my child. Ultimately, my father gave me "food for thought" through a healthy discussion on the gift of "free choice" and the consequences of our decisions.

    I've always known my father to be an intelligent, compassionate man of discernment, but during that traumatic time in my family's life, his anger preceded his logic and compassion. I later discovered that when my father learned of the statutory rape of his virgin fourteen-year-old middle child by a man of twenty-two years of age, he was livid and made various attempts to take legal action through the court system, but to no avail. Fortunately, no illegal action followed. My understanding today is that my father's anger was so enraging that he and my older brother went looking for Myishia's father to teach him a lesson. Through God's good grace, they were unable to locate him as a different outcome may have affected all of us in my family. In my mind, considering my father's rage, someone was going to get injured or end up in jail. In retrospect, I believe my father felt violated, devalued, and disrespected as a man and father. However, in order to have a future with his family, he had to learn to move out of his own way and let it go.

After much soul-searching and discernment regarding the option of adoption or foster care, my godmother was the catalyst to an encouraging decision. She helped me to understand the consequence of my decision to place my daughter up for adoption. Once I processed her advice, I felt that the legal written contract of adoption would be too final, rigid, and conclusive. I knew if I gave up my daughter, I would spend the rest of my life looking for her. I therefore chose not to give my daughter up for adoption. Even at fifteen years old, I could not imagine the idea of never seeing my child again. Instead, I chose the foster home option.

Since I was still in high school, arrangements were made for Myishia to be placed for one year in a catholic adoption agency called "The Angel Guardian Home for Little Children" located in the Bay Ridge area of Brooklyn, New York. Much to my dismay, during her confinement, I was not able to bring her home for visits with me. However, I intermittently stayed connected with her through visits on my own. This adoption agency was also responsible for foster care placements for their residents. Subsequently, Myishia was fortunate enough to be placed in a foster home in St. Albans, New York until the age of three. Under this new arrangement, I was able to bring her home for visits with me almost weekly.

The Right Choice

Because I was so young, I constantly evaluated my neophyte motherly instincts. Sometimes it was difficult to travel from my house to the foster home where she stayed, but I always made the effort. Since I didn't have a car and no one in my family had a car, I either traveled for more than an hour by subway or a neighbor would supportively drive me. Apparently, my visits to Myishia and the bond we created were of great value to her. Looking back, I'm so grateful I made those visits. My plan was to bring Myishia home for good when she was three years old when I was due to finish high school. Unfortunately, when I became eighteen, I did not graduate with my class because I failed history. Consequently, another significant and life-changing choice had to be made! I could either stay in school for six more months or drop out. My final decision was to drop out of high school. I had made a promise to myself to independently care for my daughter by the time she was three years old. I desperately wanted to live up to this commitment.

My Maternal Instincts

"Children, obey your parents in everything, for this pleases the Lord."
Colossians 3:20

Unlike many mother-daughter teenage relationships today, Myishia clearly trusted me and would share with me her deepest fears until she was eighteen. Up until that time, we openly discussed issues at school, relationships with boys, bullies and other challenges. The level of trust we established as mother and daughter was because of our open communication process and my candidness with her as her mother. This channel of communication was a conscious choice on my part as my greatest fear was that she would hear from the outside world information about her past. Specifically, I wanted her to hear from me that she was born out of wedlock and that her stepfather was not her biological father. I therefore shared this information with her when she was about seven years old.

My maternal instinct was to protect her because I didn't want her to make the same mistakes I made by not having a confidante or someone to talk with. However, throughout our mother-daughter bond, she never shared with me her feelings and confusion about her sexual orientation. She later revealed to me that she was afraid I would disown her and perhaps send her back to that dark place of pain, the foster home. I was shocked that she had these kinds of thoughts, but certainly understood.

Remember, I carried Myishia for nine months without revealing my situation to anyone. I too was afraid I would be disowned.

My Daughter's Secret

As a child, I believe Myishia instinctively knew that her grandfather, my father, was also a same-gender loving man. Uncle Joe and her grandfather were partners and in a live-in relationship from the time Myishia was born in 1958 up until my father's death in 1975. She readily gravitated to both of them. Perhaps because of my denial, I never thought that this special bond with her grandfather would have been a source of belonging and support for my daughter. As expressed earlier, I never suspected Myishia inherited this same-gender loving gene until she was about eighteen. Actually, it took this number of years for her to reveal to me her internal struggle and confusion that revolved around her sexual status. Years later she explained that she didn't want to disappoint me by speaking to this inner struggle of being different. She was also fearful of my response to her dilemma thinking that I will abandon her and send her back to foster care.

Regrettably and retrospectively, I discovered later in life, her pain was so great that by the time she was fifteen, she resorted to sneaking glasses of alcohol from our liquor cabinet. Since my husband and I only consumed alcohol when we entertained, we never monitored our stock of liquor. Her use of alcohol escalated later in life into a alcohol and drug addiction. Her enigmatic behavior became evident in high school when I was called to speak with the school psychologist. This was when I heard the devastating news that Myishia had attempted suicide. Apparently, a few days before, while I was working, she tried to cut her wrists. Fortunately, she didn't penetrate her skin, but the marks were obvious to her concerned teacher who took notice. Prior to this meeting, I was ignorant to Myishia's on-going pain and attempt on her life. As her busy working mother, I left the house in the morning at about seven and didn't return home until after six. This incident was such a shocking revelation for me that it woke me up. I knew I had to slow down.

The Benefit of Therapy

Together, we followed through with therapy, but to no avail. Ultimately, at the recommendation of the therapist, we scheduled our visits separately. Even then, Myishia never revealed the internal struggle she was having living a lie as a same-gender loving teenager, not even to her therapist. She gave other reasons for attempting her life. She didn't trust the therapist or me. When we were together in the sessions as a threesome, she was very unresponsive. I'm not sure what happened when I was not there with Myishia and the therapist. However, today I know she needed to release her hidden thoughts, guilt, and fear of letting the world know that she was gay. Today I believe if she had freed herself by *moving out of her own way* that November in 1978, some of the pain she experienced in life may have been avoided.

  As mentioned in the previous lesson, while she was in college, she ultimately revealed her sexual orientation status to me. Not knowing that she had escalated from drinking to drugging, her behavior and those of her friends were everything I detested, specifically in females. They appeared to be apathetic about their careers or future as responsible adults. I was naïve regarding their drug-induced apathy. In actuality, I was livid about her choice of friends more than her sexual orientation.

  My first thought as a mother was, "What did I do to cause this?" To clear up my confusion, for the second time, I sought and visited a clinical therapist to help me to crystalize my own thinking and feelings. My goal was to determine if I had played any part in her growth and development as a same-gender loving person. I also desperately wanted to shed any feelings of being judged as a bad mother so we could move forward and live a normal family life. After engaging in a few sessions with a certified clinical psychologist, I was relieved of any personal guilt. Even back in the seventies, research indicated that homosexuality could be environmentally oriented, but appeared to be more genetic than choice.

Thirty years later, I now know Myishia tried hard to be heterosexual. As a teenager, in order to camouflage her sexuality and please me, she dated young men who were interested in her, attended heterosexual parties, and wore the girly or sexy dresses I bought and imposed upon her. I never knew how hypocritical she felt or how miserable she really was. Once I did find out about her sexual orientation, my emotional and persistent negative response to Myishia's behavior unfortunately didn't help. It only caused her to search for a less stressful life. She simply wanted to escape from the rigidity imposed upon her by me, her mother. At that time, all I could think about were my needs. Consequently, for more than three decades, we had an erratic relationship.

What We Don't Know

I know that my father was a same-gender loving man, but what I don't know is who else in previous generations perhaps "closet homosexuals" were. How far back is the root of this genetic behavior? I also know that in my current family generation, there are quite a few same-gender loving relatives who we love and receive unconditionally.

In February, 2014, Sarah Knapton, Science Correspondent, wrote an article on this topic. Richard Lane of Stonewall said that while studies into the origins of homosexuality have yet to produce firm evidence, they do point to a biological root. He specifically said: *"The thing that's consistent across all of them (the research) is that they all point to sexual orientation being something fundamental to a person rather than the lifestyle choice some opponents of equality suggest."* To this day, I continue to research its cause in the interest of educating others. My goal is to help others accept, love, and support same-gender loving people and their families.

A Daughter's View

"Submitting to one another out of reverence for Christ"
Ephesians 5:21

As mature adults who have overcome many obstacles as mother and daughter, Myishia revealed to me many of her feelings about her past. While in the foster home at age three, Myishia would eagerly await by the window for me to appear. She would be so excited to see me that I truly felt valued by her innocent and unadulterated love. She would run to me, hug me, and place her small hand in mine as though somehow I would disappear if she let it go. When I later questioned Myishia about this experience, she stated: "I really wanted to come home and stay with you at Maya's house; I didn't like my home in foster care and so looked forward to your arrival."

It is interesting to recall, at the immature age of fifteen, that I received no parental guidance regarding my visits to my daughter. I only know that I retrieved my daughter on weekends because my values taught me that it was the right thing to do. I was too naïve to give much thought to how she may have been treated while under the foster family's care. In retrospect, my recall is that I was never invited into the house where she stayed as a foster child. Myishia was simply passed over to me on the front porch without much of an exchange in words. Today, if I knew what I now know, I probably would have insisted in seeing her living arrangement. However, I was too young and immature to make this type of demand.

Childhood Memories

As a child, Myishia loved our large extended family. She has expressed that family has always been a refuge for her. Her recall included our most memorable family getaway, a ten-day trip to Bermuda, with her brother, aunts, cousins, and of course, me. "The moment I stepped foot onto the tarmac of the Bermuda airport, I felt at home because of our Caribbean roots. Since I was only about nine years old, being away with you and the family on this beautiful island was an amazing adventure! It was filled with so much joy, lots of sunshine, an aqua-blue ocean, powder white sand, and laughter. I was thrilled to be playing with my cousins, dancing, sightseeing and enjoying the abundance of wonderful foods. I loved it!"

The Impact of Rejection

As you can see, Myishia cherished her family. But then there came a time when she began experiencing what she perceived as rejection by the family. As a teenager and young adult, she experienced incidents of being teased, talked about, and ostracized. This is what she recalls as being the beginning of an era of rebellion and withdrawal from the family. This is when she began her painful journey of delving into active addition and retreating into herself. Eventually, at age twenty, she left home and her addiction took over her life.

Later on in her healthy life, she stated "I believe the rejection I experienced as a child, teenager, and young adult left a deeply-rooted emotional scar; my sexuality issues simply exacerbated the scar. What I do know is that I still have some magical memories of my childhood, and they are forever etched in my heart as great times! I was very fortunate as a child, and I know that now. I had a mother who loved me. I also believe, had I not been a same-gender loving woman, the impact of the family tensions would not have been as intense. I say this because I would not have been as scarred as I am today with memories of rejection. So, what I know for sure, I would not have chosen my sexual orientation, if I had the choice."

Her True Feelings

During our numerous intimate conversations, Myishia shared with me that she knew she was a same-gender loving person when she was about six years old, but did not know how to express this revelation with me. She felt that I would be disappointed in her, perhaps angry, and possibly reject her as my daughter. Consequently, she learned to internalize her feelings and thoughts about how she perceived the world around her. She revealed that she was in a tremendous amount of pain and on a slow suicide mission. Because she could not relate to how people in her era, the sixties, seventies, and eighties, felt about same-gender loving relationships, her secret life caused her to constantly experience the pain of rejection.

She felt that she simply was not good enough to be accepted by the family. She legitimized her feelings by weighing heavily on the comparison of herself with other same-gender loving people in the family. Not only was my father gay, but there were also same-gender loving family members on her stepfather's side. Her thoughts and feelings led to: "Why can't I also be accepted?"

Over the past thirty years, while we were estranged, we both have transitioned into healthier, considerate, and more understanding women. We have finally accepted each other for who we are and not who we want each other to be. Again, in one of our many intimate conversations, Myishia expressed more sentiments to me of how she felt as a three year-old while in foster care: "I realized how much I adored you, depended on you, and idolized you. You were my Goddess, my world, and my mother who loved me and rescued me from the painful, dark environment in which I lived. I didn't know I was in foster care. I just knew you were my mother and that you were consistent in coming for me. Therefore, even when I was lonely and frightened, I always had you in my head and in my heart and that I could look forward to seeing you."

With the benefit of hindsight, it gives me a warm and fuzzy feeling to know how Myishia loved me with such deference and adoration, which she still demonstrates today. I am a blessed woman. Three decades later, the love between Myishia and me has gone full circle. Over the latter part of our lives, I can honestly say we have developed a truly authentic mother and daughter bond. Because of our indelible connection, I learned more about my daughter and her plight as a same-gender loving woman than perhaps a mother of a heterosexual child may ever know about her adult child. I attribute this "Circle of Love" to me shifting my thinking to a more adaptable and affirming attitude and being able to *move out of my own way* to truly accept differences without judgment. Because we are only fifteen years apart, we have become best friends.

The Union between a Mother and Her Only Son

"She opens her mouth with wisdom and the teaching of kindness is on her tongue. She looks well to the ways of her household and does not eat the bread of idleness." Proverbs 31:26

I was more mature at age twenty when my son was born and I was thrilled by his birth. Contrary to the experiences with my first born, my daughter, I felt privileged to be able to now legally hold, nurture, and express complete love to this wonder, my newborn baby, J.R. I actually felt like a complete woman. I was older, wiser, and now married with two children. I saw us as the ideal family.

So many things were happening when J.R. was introduced to his new environment. I was a newlywed, still enamored with my first love, and while quite happy, somewhat vulnerable in this new relationship. My contentment was a result of finally feeling independent. Similar to my mother's experience, this was my first home as a married woman, away from siblings and my mother.

On the contrary, Gary's mother, grandmother, and siblings lived directly across the street from us. To me, he was simply my husband and authentic father of my son and stepfather to my daughter. We were a family! I never gave thought to the impact the proximity of his family could have had on his sphere of influence as a man, a husband, or a father.

Today, because of the relationship with my own son, I now know that mothers have a foremost and lasting effect in their son's lives. When Gary and I married, and he became a father for the first time, he was still his mother's son. He was consistently under his mother's influence and unspoken expectations throughout our marriage.

A Mother's View of Her Only Son

"And blessed is she who believed that there would be a fulfillment of what was spoken to her from the Lord." Luke 1:45

Unlike my experience with my first child, I recall being elated to be on maternity leave for four months: one month prior to my son's birth, and three months before reentering the workplace. I now had the opportunity to nurture both my five-year old daughter, as well as learn how to be the perfect mother of my newborn child. Unfortunately, the best-laid plans went awry. One week after J.R. was born, and for about six weeks thereafter, I became critically ill with a kidney infection. Suddenly and alarmingly, I found myself in a sexist and emotionally abusive relationship. I was very ill and was devastated when I found that I did not have the support I expected. Therefore, although ill, I still managed to wake up every four hours to change diapers, feed, and nurture J.R. as best I could. This was not a good time for me psychologically or emotionally in my new marriage. Although I was only in my first year of marriage, I felt very much alone and helpless during this ordeal. This was the beginning of my authentic introduction to my own distorted view of love and marriage. At the young age of twenty, each page turned revealed another unexpected occurrence, emotion, and consequence.

As a toddler, J.R. became so attached to me that he would scream and holler whenever I transferred him into the arms of a relative, other than his father. He was truly an affectionate child, filled with passion and many emotions. He was also highly intelligent, talked fast, walked fast, and had other idiosyncrasies that I later discovered were associated with a latent mental illness. The biggest indicator that there might be some form of psychosis going on with him was his resistance to having any form of food touch other food on his plate. He was about three years old when I noticed this consistent behavior, which ultimately prevailed into his adult years. He was also obsessive about time. Being late for anything was not an option for him. He was obviously disturbed whenever this need to be on time was threatened or compromised. However, my perception of him was that he was just my son who had a unique but loving personality.

J.R. openly demonstrated his love for me with kisses, hugs, and sentiments of affection until he was about twelve years old. As though it was yesterday, I clearly recall a shift in his affectionate behavior toward me. His body language and words of resistance told me a lot about what he was thinking. He didn't want his friends to see me give my usual goodbye kiss when sending him off to school, camp, or church. He was evolving into a young man with his own thoughts about manhood! Actually, he was a leader similar to my oldest brother, Malvane, who inspired a host of friends to follow him. Like his dad, J.R. was handsome, gregarious, funny, spontaneous, and fanatically sports-oriented. Before this halting transition began, J.R. would openly express his love for me by saying the words: "I love you, Mom." One day, when he was about five years old, walking with him hand in hand, he proclaimed he wanted to marry me when he grew up. So, again I say, the first time I felt truly loved was reiterated by my children. To this day, J.R. is still very expressive and affectionate in demonstrating his love for me. In retrospect, until his mood swings began, what was there not to like?

The Abuse

The first time I experienced bodily mishandling by anyone in my young life was by my first husband who, during one of his mood swings, struck me when I was seven-months pregnant. Considering I was so close to giving birth, I was shocked by his physical response to my naiveté or candor. I was accustomed to his mood swings, but this physical attack was the first.

Due to the impact of his assault, I fell backward and hit the bedpost. Carrying a fetus, I often wondered whether J.R. was somehow affected by this trauma. I was raised in a home where my parents never harmed me with malice. I don't even recall my father ever hitting me. I can only remember one time where my mother spanked me with a belt for disobedience when I was about eight. That was not my mother's style, so I felt that I probably deserved it. I have never been a victim of violence in my young life, so this act of abuse was disturbing for me and would stay with me for many years to come. As time moved on and as people in love may do, I forgave Gary for striking me and prayed it would not happen again. I wanted my marriage to work.

A Pattern of Dysfunctional Behavior

The second time I was threatened and emotionally abused by Gary was when J.R. was about three months old. At about ten o'clock one summer night, J.R. was quickly dressed, wrapped in blankets, and swiftly taken from his bassinette by his angry father. I was intimidated, bewildered, hysterical and beside myself with worry and astonishment. I cried, screamed, pleaded with J.R.'s father to not make a point that he was in complete control of me by using our child as a pawn. Gary ignored my pleas and walked out of the door with our son in his arms. For the first time since I brought J.R. home from the hospital, he was separated from me. I did not call the police as, based on my values, I considered this abduction to be a family matter.

In the black community, our acculturation was not to involve officials of the law into a family situation unless it was life threatening. The conditioning was that the police could make matters worse for the perpetrator. He was my husband and my baby's father; I wanted no harm to come to either of them. Rather, I chose to anxiously wait for their return.

About two hours later, Gary returned home with J.R. in his arms without a word of apology or explanation. To this day, I don't know where my son was taken. I was just grateful to God that he was returned unharmed. As a mother, this was probably one of the worst two hours of my life. Again I wonder, although just an infant, how was J.R. affected by this impact?

You see, this was just the beginning of a pattern of systematic physical and emotional incidents in our household. My children and I were ridiculed, humiliated and abandoned on more than one occasion. This was the beginning of a sporadic pattern of Gary's mood swings and behavioral problems that I was not aware of prior to marriage. Even when he struck me for the first time during my pregnancy, I was in denial. Mental health issues were not on the radar in my community at that time.

The Exit Strategy

I separated from Gary when Myishia was fourteen and J.R. was nine. Gary and I were at a get-together one night when, due to a jealous rage, one of his more frequent mood-swings surfaced. He became overbearing by following me around and making curt remarks. By the end of the evening, we had disrupted the party through a public display that resulted in a physical exchange. This was the beginning phase of developing my exit strategy. I knew without a doubt that I wanted out of this marriage! Immediately, the wheels started turning.

Within the year, I secretly researched and applied for a three-bedroom, two-bathroom apartment in a new high rise in the Bronx, called Co-op City. I then revealed to my father, who unfortunately was terminally ill and hospitalized at the time, my plan for a separation. His immediate response was, "I have never in the all years that you've been married to Gary seen your husband show any affection towards you in my presence." He understood my plight and was happy to help me financially. His generosity and unconditional love ultimately changed my life. Where would I be today, if he had not supported me? My sister

Roberta was always an unwavering support system and was with me through the ups and downs of this life-changing decision, including the actual relocation. I subsequently contacted and hired a moving company, gathered my children and moved to a new location and a new life. I was excited to begin entering a phase in my life as a single mother, living in an upscale urban community, which was very different from my past suburban experiences.

However, I ran into a few snags. To my dismay, my nine-year old son J.R. preferred to stay with his father. The realization that my baby boy rejected me was emotionally and psychologically overwhelming. The separation from J.R. lasted for just under five months but his absence seemed like five years to me.

The Impact Point

I thought I knew my children until I approached this crossroad that required me and my children to make a choice about our destiny. I believe this was an impact point in all of our lives. Disappointedly, I discovered that J.R.'s loyalty to family was more with his dad than with his mom. I felt that I had been stabbed repeatedly in my heart, as I was heartbroken when he made that choice. It is unfortunate that a decision like this even had to occur for this nine-year old who loved us both. However, I was devastated. J.R. chose to stay with his father rather than come with me and his sister. He ended up staying with his father for about five months until he realized the distinct differences in behavior between his mother and father. As part of Gary's personality, it was difficult for him to express verbal love, affection, or words of affirmation to J.R., Myishia, or even to me. By contrast, I verbally expressed my love and affection to my children, as well as my husband. After months of absence of affection, J.R. decided to join Myishia and me in our new environment; he needed to feel valued once again. After his return, we never really talked about his experience with his father.

Myishia, being the free spirit she is, could see no other way in life except to stay with her mother. She was then and still is my rock. This was a difficult time in all of our lives as we now moved to another borough, a high-rise instead of a house, and to a predominately Jewish community. My children had to meet the challenges of establishing new friends and adapting to the public school system, as well as the Jewish culture. Prior to this impactful transition in their young lives, they had always attended parochial schools. Now they were educated in the public school system. In retrospect, I acknowledge that this separation had to be a traumatic transition for both of them. Subsequently, we were separated as a family unit for approximately one year from my husband and J.R.'s father. Later in life these feelings of abandonment, divisiveness, and confusion were described by J.R. as yet another impact point in his young life.

Although his father was never diagnosed with a mental illness, I believe my son inherited this disorder from his father and his family's genetic history. Over the years Gary's mother as well as his sister were both hospitalized on several occasions and diagnosed with mental disabilities. Thirty-five years after leaving his father for the first time, my son also became a target for clinical depression and mental illness. At age forty-two, he was diagnosed with Borderline Personality Disorder and bi-polar II.

The Symptoms

As previously mentioned, I began to notice some unusual behavior about J.R. when he was about three years old. J.R. would get very upset if his food would touch other food on his plate. As he got older, he also had emotional outbursts when given a directive, challenging me with, "Just because you are my mother, you can't tell me what to do!" This challenging attitude began when he was about twelve. Being punctual, which is not a bad thing, was also part of his compulsive behavior.

In contrast to his sister, Myishia, he never had to be coached to leave the house on time for school. Because he walked the three blocks to school every day in elementary, middle, and high school, he factored in enough time so he was never late. In actuality, he was a good student. When I asked J.R. about his school experience, he said, "I can't explain why, but I still have vivid memories of my early school days. I never felt like I was better than anyone else, but knew I was as smart if not smarter. I remember my teacher always saying to me, "You get by without even trying or applying yourself." This speaks to his high IQ.

His True Feelings

He did say, however, that he never felt loved by anyone in the household except by me, his mother. Through our mother-son adult dialogue regarding his childhood, he revisited the emptiness he experienced with his father by not ever hearing the words "I love you, son". He knew that his father was not a man who felt comfortable expressing his feelings to anyone in an affirming way, but that did not ease the void. Retrospectively, J.R. and his father did lack a genuine "father and son" relationship. Although they were both avid sports fans and watched games together on television, they did not create a bond where they could talk intimately to each other as confidants. His father was very strict, regimented, and moody. These elements also did not help in the relationship.

His True Character

During this part of his life's journey, he also discovered that loyalty was part of his DNA. Most of his friends were moving from one girl to another and enjoying their young single life. However, J.R. chose not to get on this bandwagon. Again, it resonated for him that he was different! At age fifteen, he began a seven-year romantic relationship which ended when he was twenty-two. He said, "I was, for the most part, loyal in my relationship as seven years is a long time." There were times when I witnessed his happiness with his girlfriend, but also observed many times of discontent.

The Primary Trigger

My one and only grandchild was a result of this seven-year union and one of the reasons for their ultimate break-up. His girlfriend loved J.R. very much and was hopeful they would ride any storm together, marry, and live happily ever after. Unfortunately, their daughter, Jamie, was diagnosed with Osteogenesis Imperfecta (OI), which is a rare brittle bone disease. Jamie was very tiny when she was born, less than four pounds and about fifteen inches long. Had her mother not had a cesarean, Jamie never would have survived being delivered through the birth canal. However, when Jamie was surgically removed from her mother's uterus and abdomen, almost every bone in her small frame was either broken or fractured.

My fiancé and I were sitting in the waiting room when we received this devastating news. The expression on J.R.'s face gave it away. He was in total shock. When I went into the delivery room to see my grandchild, I understood his shocking expression. Jamie was not only tiny but looked distorted with a pointy chest, and wrapped almost from neck to feet with gauze and bandages. I could not believe this was happening. As a young man, again the trigger was touched when he became a father of his physically challenged daughter.

I, too, was hurt and emotionally beside myself when her incurable condition was digested. I actually looked forward to being a grandmother. This was my first and only grandchild and prior to her birth, my prayer was she would have a long and fulfilling normal life, and my fiancé and I would be an integral part of it. This episode in J.R's life was one of the initial causes in the surfacing of his latent Borderline Personality Disorder (BPD).

The Challenging Breakup

Together with J.R. and Jamie's mother, Cheryl, we had quite a few conferences at the hospital with Jamie's physician about her condition, prognosis, and recommendations. He warned them that her condition could have an adverse impact on their current relationship as parents and as a couple. He eventually recommended that Jamie be placed in an institution where she would receive proper care. Admirably, this was not acceptable by Jamie's mother. She decided to hire the necessary nurses and other health care professionals to help her independently raise or care for her child.

As each year passed, unfortunately, the doctor was right. This was a devastating experience for J.R., Cheryl and, of course, Jamie. The issues were just too great for them to manage; the strain financially, psychologically, and emotionally tore their ten-year relationship apart. They ultimately made a conscious choice to go their separate ways. In the end, J.R.'s daughter and my only granddaughter passed away at age seven as a result of the disease. Up until her transition, J.R. consistently paid monthly child support toward his daughter's well-being. To this day, I still commend Cheryl for her courage to fight for her child and personally nurture her daughter until the end.

J.R.'s Perplexing Maturation Journey

First and foremost, as I understand it today, J.R.'s emotional triggers began as a child with the divorce between his mother and father, which rocked his world. As the years passed,

J.R.'s many impulsive decisions led to choices that resulted in mostly negative consequences. This included enlisting in the US Army where he was placed on medical leave due to pneumonia during boot camp. When he recuperated after a few weeks in the hospital, he was told he had to start boot camp from the beginning. He therefore chose the option not to return.

Subsequently, J.R. enrolled in a State College in Virginia and ultimately left in his first semester year due to what he perceived as administrative challenges. His expectation was that college life would be more organized by those in authority. He eventually became extremely frustrated with the violation of his expectations.

Next, at age twenty-two, he experienced an impetuous relationship which led to a six-week marriage with his first wife which was just as quickly annulled. While still in a vulnerable state after the annulment, he met and married, for the second time, a woman who knocked at his door to promote the Jehovah Witness ministry.

July 17, 1996, was a shocking day for J.R. On this very day, two devastating events occurred. Not only was it the day that TWA Flight 800 blew up over the Long Island Sound, eleven minutes after take-off, killing everyone onboard including more than 250 passengers, he was confronted at the door by his wife with an overwhelming confession. Still jolted by the impact of the airline disaster, he learned from his wife of ten years that she had been engaged in an ongoing, one-year affair with J.R.'s father, my ex-husband, Gary. This was a shattering betrayal and it irrevocably breached J.R.'s trust. It was also a shock to all of us in the family since the belief he had in his wife was rated just as high as he had for his father. This incident resulted in a number of consequences: a physical altercation between J.R. and Gary; the excommunication of his wife from the Jehovah Witness Kingdom Hall; and still another major setback in my son's young life. This was an added activated trigger that tapped on the head of this sleeping mental illness called Borderline Personality Disorder or BPD!

Due to this divorce, he was a single man again. Eventually, he remarried for the third time and stayed in that relationship for ten years. However, while maintaining his marital relationship and a record of seventeen years at the same New York City organization, J.R. had another unexpected trigger that was tapped just a wee bit too hard.

The Breaking Point

The last and most devastating trigger was when J.R. was psychologically and emotionally victimized as an eyewitness to the September 11th World Trade Center attack. At age thirty-six, the post-traumatic stress of this experience was his breaking point. During that dreadful day, J.R. was in a state of panic. Neither he nor his coworkers knew what had happened as midtown was thrown into a state of chaos. Even the leaders in the organization were at a loss in knowing what to communicate to their staff. Also, amidst all of the confusion, he could not contact or locate his wife. When they finally did connect, they, along with thousands of people employed in Midtown Manhattan, covered in soot, walked for hours before reaching their homes.

Roland and I were living in Georgia when we received this unexpected early morning call from J.R. We had not as yet turned on the television, so we had no knowledge of what was happening on the northeastern coast. Hearing my son's voice frightened me. I immediately became concerned for his life when he told me that two separate planes hit each one of the Twin Towers, known as the tallest buildings in the world from 1971 to 1973. At this point, we were not aware that we were literally attacked by terrorists. Subsequently, Roland and I watched in horror as the twin towers burned. We saw people jumping to their death from infernal windows and running through the streets in panic and fear. Finally, we watched as these tall, world-famous buildings, one by one, collapsed. Of course, the rest is history.

  Consequently, this latest incident as an eyewitness to this horrific event led J.R. to making the decision to leave New York, the only home he knew, and settle in Atlanta, Georgia. However, it took four years to finally make this move. The company he worked for was relocating to Charlotte, North Carolina and they made him an offer to join them. Because he wanted to be closer to family, he declined and instead he and his wife decided to move to Atlanta. After arriving here with his wife, using their life savings to purchase a house, as well as to establish their own business of a limousine service, his optimistic plans didn't go as expected. In addition to adapting to a different culture, there were just too many triggers that surfaced. He was a first-time homeowner, facing many twists and turns that he was not financially prepared to meet. He was a Jehovah Witness at the time and believed that his wife should not work. This alone caused anxiety and stress. He also experienced state-law restrictions regarding his start-up limousine service that also increased his level of anxiety.

Additionally, for the first time in his life, he experienced job challenges in the south that he never experienced in the northeast. New York is a democratic or "blue" state. Atlanta, Georgia is a very progressive, "red" or republican state requiring a shift in mindset to understand and to adapt to the differences in regional culture.

A Son's View

"And behold, a voice from heaven said, "This is my beloved son, with whom I am well pleased." Matthew 3:17

Dr. Shari Y. Manning, author of "Loving Someone with Borderline Personality Disorder (BPD)", speaks to the fact that people diagnosed with BPD generally are intelligent with a high IQ and very compassionate, loving people and animals. She specifically says:

"People with BPD were born with an invisible, innate difference that profoundly changed the landscape for them when they were growing up. She also says, "It takes two basic ingredients and time to make BPD. The first ingredient is an innate, biological vulnerability to emotions…The second ingredient is an invalidating environment, and time is what pulls the two ingredients together. So when we talk about an invalidating environment that contributes to BPD, we generally mean the environment in which the person grew up."

The First Ingredient: An Inherent Vulnerability to Emotions

J.R. always demonstrated a character that was funny, inquisitive, mischievous, passionate, gregarious, smart, and loyal.

He also loved people and knew how to show empathy when he felt someone was being mistreated. He definitely had a personality where people consistently gravitated toward him. Yet, he said he always knew he was different. As his mother, I also knew he was different, but never associated his differences with a mental disorder. He was just comically unique, adventurous, and loved to laugh and have fun.

There is a five-year difference between J.R. and his sister, Myishia. She was fourteen and he was nine when our family fell apart. I was the one who sat them down together around the kitchen table to share the disparaging news of our pending separation. Myishia was quiet, while J.R. had many questions about our future. He was always an inquisitive and emotional child. "What will happen to us?" "Where will we live?" "What about my friends? Will I ever see them again?" "Where will I go to school?" And finally, "What will happen to Daddy?" While I made every effort to respond to each of his reasonable questions, he was not a happy camper.

Although J.R. was only nine years old at the time, this was the beginning stage of recognizing his latent mental state of BPD that sometimes led to unexplainable outbursts. According to J.R.'s recall, the process of hearing the news from me that his father and I were getting a divorce was when his life changed and became an impact point in his life. He felt abandoned and hopeless. Even today, neither one of us are sure whether his decision to live with his father was to hurt me for interfering with his predictable and secure world or because he was not willing to let go of his stable world that included his father.

Remember what Dr. Manning spoke on regarding acquiring BPD. "It takes <u>two basic ingredients and *time*</u> to make

BPD. The first ingredient is an innate, biological vulnerability to emotions…The second ingredient is an invalidating environment, and *time* is what pulls the two ingredients together."

When I probed J.R. about his teenage years, he revealed that it was in this stage of his life that he began questioning his emotions, behavior, and thinking. He believes that drinking beer at an early age, fourteen or fifteen years old, was definitely a trigger. He also realized that his emotions took over at age seventeen when he punched his fist through a closet door in our home. This was the first of many similar incidents of an uncontrollable temper.

One particular night, I put him out of the house because of his demonstrated disrespect toward me. I had a rule that if you had a job, which he did, it was a family requirement or value to contribute a small portion to the household. I was raised this way and passed this value on to my children. He was very upset with me because I placed this demand on him. He considered this request to be unreasonable and didn't want to follow it. Subsequently, I immediately demanded that he leave, as I would not tolerate disrespect from him or anyone else anymore. This caused an emotional outburst, where he slammed his fist into the wall with such force that it caused severe damage to the wall and pain and swelling to his hand. When he attempted to reappear later that night, through tears and hurt, I refused to let him return. It was important for me as his mother to educate him on the consequences associated with devaluing respect for your elders or authority, especially a parent. Despite my pain of rejecting him in the moment, my intent was not to harm him, but to help him in his future choices. He later told me he stayed in a stairwell all night and realized his emotions were out of control to which he apologized. In retrospect, he said this level of discipline was one of the most valuable lessons of his life. He learned the importance of self-respect and what people who respect themselves will do to maintain it. He saw my tears and knew I was deeply hurt by our mother-son bout. He also knew I loved him and that I believed in tough love. Therefore, he understood that my decision to deny his re-entrance back into our home was as painful for me as it was for him.

The Second Ingredient: The Impact of an Invalidating Environment

As discussed earlier, I believed my dysfunctional marital experiences with J.R.'s father adversely obstructed both of my children's childhood development, ultimately leading to an "invalidating environment". However, in speaking to J.R. about his adult views on his childhood, he disagreed. J.R. described his experience at home a little different from my perspective. He did not feel he came from an invalidating environment, but rather a relatively happy, fulfilling, and family-oriented home, until the divorce. He especially enjoyed the holidays where he spent jubilant times with his aunts, uncles, and many cousins on Thanksgiving, Christmas, and Easter Sunday. Apparently our holidays were special to both Myishia and J.R. If you will recall, Myishia also spoke of the ecstatic holidays in the same sentiment. Nonetheless, the invalidating environment began with the divorce.

The Third Ingredient: Time

When the first ingredient to Borderline Personality Disorder emerged, "acknowledgement of his emotions", it was simply the initial stage of BPD. The second ingredient was the result of the "invalidating environment" and the culmination of his past experiences, both short and long term, in New York as well as Atlanta, Georgia. It actually took about thirty-six years for my son's latent mental health battle to finally surface full-blown. I was called to his home by his wife one afternoon, stating that J.R. took an overdose of pills and was cutting up his arms and chest with a kitchen knife. Of course, upon my arrival, the police had also been contacted and J.R. was immediately admitted to a mental health facility for seven days. Since this was a perceived attempted suicide, he was evaluated and ultimately diagnosed with Borderline Personality Disorder. When I asked J.R. how he felt about this diagnosis, he simply said, "Relieved." He said he knew something was wrong, but didn't know how to describe it.

Consequently, the culmination of all these dysfunctional events happening one after another produced his innate, biological vulnerability to emotions to rear its ugly head. As you can see, the aforementioned two ingredients and the addition of "time" was the beginning of his journey into the world of mental illness that took over his life.

Knowledge is Power

So, what is J.R.'s message to you, the reader, in giving me permission to so honestly reveal his lifecycle, the choices he's made, his triggers, sharing the few attempts to end his life, and his ultimate diagnosis? He believes that knowledge is power and simply wants you to know in his own words that Borderline Personality Disorder is treatable! "I am relieved that I had the opportunity to be diagnosed and treated. It will still rear its ugly head from time to time, but *it is* treatable. I no longer have the life that I once had, but I'm alive. With life, there is always hope. Now I have to make it a life worth living!"

As J.R.'s mother, I truly believe that if I am going to *move out of my own way* and live a life worth living, I need to be of value to my son. I also must consider other loved ones, friends, or relatives with diagnosed or undiagnosed BPD, Bipolar, or its outgrowth. I therefore have decided to commit to first and foremost educating myself on its symptoms and treatment that can be helpful to others.

I do know people who have been diagnosed with clinical depression, bi-polar, and BPD. I also know people who may not have been diagnosed with a mental health challenge, but in whom the dysfunctional symptoms are evident to me. Therefore, if I want to be supportive to the mentally challenged community who are being treated or not treated, my mission is to educate others by removing the stigma that people with BPD, bi-polar depression, or other forms of non-functional treatable mental illness are facing today.

As a starting point, below is a brief overview from the National Education Alliance, Borderline Personality Disorder, which may be helpful:

What is Borderline Personality Disorder?

Borderline personality disorder (BPD) is a serious mental illness that causes unstable moods, behavior, and relationships. It usually begins during adolescence or early adulthood.

What do most people who have BPD suffer from?

Problems regulating their emotions and thoughts
Impulsive and sometimes reckless behavior
Unstable Relationships Incidence
BPD affects 5.9% of adults (about 14 million Americans) at some time in their life
BPD affects 50% more people than Alzheimer's disease and nearly as many as schizophrenia and bipolar combined (2.25%).
BPD affects 20% of patients admitted to psychiatric hospitals
BPD affects 10% of people in outpatient mental health treatment.

What is the Prognosis?

Research has shown that outcomes can be quite good for people with BPD, particularly if they are engaged in treatment. With specialized therapy, most people with borderline personality disorder find their symptoms are reduced and their lives are improved. Although not all the symptoms may ease, there is often a major decrease in problem behaviors and suffering. Under stress, some symptoms may come back. When this happens, people with BPD should return to therapy and other kinds of support. Many individuals with BPD experience a decrease in their impulsive behavior in their forties.

What is the Diagnosis?

A mental health professional experienced in diagnosing and treating mental disorders, such as a psychiatrist, psychologist, clinical social worker, or psychiatric nurse, can detect BPD based on:

1. An in-person interview to discuss symptoms.
2. Input from a family or close friend that adds to the information provided by the individual coming for treatment.
3. A careful and thorough medical exam can help rule out other possible causes of symptoms.

Can People be Misdiagnosed?

Unfortunately, BPD is too often misdiagnosed. Some people who have borderline personality disorder are misdiagnosed with bipolar disorder. There are important differences between these conditions but both involve unstable moods. For the person with bipolar disorder, the mood changes exist for weeks or even months. The mood changes in BPD are much shorter and are often within a day.

To be diagnosed with BPD, a person must experience at least five of the following symptoms:

Fear of abandonment
Unstable or changing relationships
Unstable self-image; struggles with identity or sense of self
Impulsive or self-damaging behaviors (e.g., excessive spending, unsafe sex, substance abuse, reckless driving, binge eating).
Suicidal behavior or self-injury
Varied or random mood swings
Constant feelings of worthlessness or sadness
Problems with anger, including frequent loss of temper or physical fights
Stress-related paranoia or loss of contact with reality

What Causes Borderline Personality Disorder?

Research on the causes and risk factors for BPD is still in its early stages. However, scientists generally agree that genetic and environmental influences are likely to be involved.

Imaging studies in people with BPD have shown abnormalities in brain structure and function, evidence that biology is a factor. In people with BPD, more activity than usual has been seen in the parts of the brain that control feeling and expressing emotions.

Certain events during childhood may also play a role in the development of the disorder, such as those involving emotional, physical and sexual abuse. Loss, neglect and bullying may also contribute. The current theory is that some people are more likely to develop BPD due to their biology or genetics and harmful childhood experiences can further increase the risk.

What are Co-morbidities?

Borderline personality disorder often occurs with other illnesses. This can make it hard to diagnose, especially if symptoms of other illnesses overlap with the BPD symptoms.

Women with BPD are more likely to have co-occurring disorders such as major depression, anxiety disorders, substance abuse or eating disorders. In men, BPD is more likely to accompany disorders such as substance abuse or antisocial personality disorder. According to the NIMH-funded National Comorbidity Survey Replication—the largest national study to date of mental disorders in U.S. adults—about 85 percent of people with BPD also suffer from another mental illness.

If you know of anyone who has been diagnosed with clinical depression, Borderline Personality Disorder (BPD), bipolar, or schizophrenia, recognize that support more than fear is needed. Each one of these mental health issues are treatable with medication, individual therapy, and support groups, but in order to be effective, it requires the support of family, friends, and a validating environment.

> Bringing the gifts that my ancestors gave, I am the dream and the hope of the slave. I Rise. I Rise. I Rise.
>
> **Maya Angelou**

Lesson Three

Seeking Love: The Journey of Anticipation

"Anyone who does not know love does not know God, because God is love."
John 4:8

    Some of us seek love to feel attractive and respected which ultimately enhances our level of self-esteem. Some of us seek love simply to fervently fulfill the void correlated with loneliness. Others seek love merely to experience the euphoria everyone is talking about. I sought love primarily to feel valued as an adult by another adult and to share my life with my soul mate forever.

    All of my pre-adult life, I received messages that I am to share my existence with another human being. I felt constantly impeached with questions such as: "Do you have a boyfriend yet?" "Are you married?" "I have a friend whom I would like for you to meet!" I also heard messages of influence regarding women and the importance of marriage as a goal in life. In my household and upbringing, specifically if you were a female, more emphasis was placed on getting married rather than attending college and earning a degree.

    Once I physically, spiritually, and emotionally progressed from my adolescent years to my teenage years and eventually to my young adult years, I maintained this conscious level of motivation. My dream was to share my eternal life with a person who would fulfill my intrinsic need to be loved and for me to give love in return. I was actually hopeful and excited in preparing myself for the day when I would meet the person who would amicably have similar needs and wants that I have and differences that balance out my deficits.

The Mystery of Love

"Two are better than one, because they have a good reward for their toil.
Ecclesiastes 4:9 ESV

Based on the number of love stories I had seen and heard, I believed that love would meet all of my needs. I was not sure of whom I was looking for in my *life partner*, but I knew I would know him when I found him. I knew I would be filled with this integral emotion called "love" that made me tingle all over whenever I would speak his name.

In meeting my presumed *life partner* for the first time, I had the choice to satisfy my needs and pursue my dreams through this person's magnetic attraction or I could simply look elsewhere. Prior to making that momentous decision to be with this special person forever, many unique feelings surfaced in me. My immediate and impassioned response to him was to savor in the moment, anticipate a future, and embrace that this euphoric feeling of joy, excitement and contentment was real and would continue forever.

I was sixteen and dating my high school sweetheart, Gary, when I believed this desire was met. He was six feet- two inches tall, athletic, personable, quite handsome, and two years older than me. These attributes embodied the fantasy that I thought my future husband would be. We dated for three years and fell in love. Once the shared mystique of our relationship became apparent, the core feelings that he was my presumed *life partner* were validated. We developed a relationship based on friendship, similar values, and our magnetic attraction to each other.

This was subsequently followed by an engagement at age eighteen and marriage at age nineteen. It was then, after the modest wedding celebration, the local honeymoon, and return to normalcy, that I crossed the threshold into the daunting reality of marriage and parenthood.

My "Free Choice" Prerogative

"Beloved, let us love one another, for love is from God, and whoever loves has been born of God and knows God. 1 John 4:7

In a conscious state, I made a life-changing decision to marry, knowing that I had options lingering in the cloud of possibilities of the unknown. "Is this the one...or should I wait?" To the contrary, I also had the option or choice to discard my responsiveness or sensation to this person's charisma and make a conscious choice to move on. However, my passion or desire for love superseded my logic and the lucidity of conscious choice disintegrated.

Specifically, prior to my first marriage, I failed to use my free choice map of possibilities, which was yet to be explored. Based on my values regarding the emotional need to enter into the sacrament of marriage, I was in a hurry to actualize my dream of being with my *life partner*. What attracted me to marriage was the whole notion of love and how it made me feel. Nothing else seemed to matter. What got in my way to being more practical, however, were the external appearances and words of affirmation that blurred my logic. I was so in love with "love" that I did not explore the core characteristics of my potential life-long mate. Therefore, I lost sight of the importance of my *life partner's* human qualities, such as his level of integrity, ethics or principles.

Unfortunately, like the majority of us who married young, I simply was not intellectually, emotionally, or psychologically prepared for what was to come once I found my *presumed life-long partner*. While I was in the throes of making a decision of the heart during this grand and necessary emotional state called love, I was fused with passion and thoughts of grandeur, sanguinity, and optimism.

Feeling Naive in My First Marriage

During this first marriage, I was guilty of the common trait of accepting subservience as a given rather than standing up for my rights as a strong, intelligent, and caring wife, mother, daughter, sister, and friend. I simply was not self-aware. I truly exemplified disrespect for myself through my meekness, passivity, and acquiescent response to my nineteen-year marriage. Disrespecting myself to this extent gave sanction to my husband and others to also overlook my intrinsic needs.

Today, I appreciate that I was more *"in love with love"* than with the man with whom I became involved, professed love for, and ultimately married. Subsequently, I learned the hard way that this magical, mystical, and sometimes dreamlike emotional state of mind that many of us experience as "love" has caused me to make poor or far-reaching choices that have had an unfavorable or long-term force on my entire life!

Consequently, during this marriage, I developed a low self-esteem persona, which in due course, through self-examination, motivated me to *move out of my own way* and turn my life around.

Married Life and Unspoken Expectations

During my first year of marriage, in 1963, I continued to be employed. Throughout the sixties, it was customary for wives who were mothers to work. This was the beginning of the era of two-income families, latch key kids, and rapid change. So, as was the new custom, six weeks after J.R. was born, I returned to work as a secretary in midtown Manhattan. As a mother of two small children, I was experiencing the financial struggles that many young couples must feel as they enter into this start-up phase of their lives. Nonetheless, as time moved on, all went well until the empty promises of eliminating emotional and physical abuse from our marriage was violated.

The marital arrangement was nothing like I expected. Somehow the love, passion, and respect we had for each other prior to marriage shifted. The unspoken expectations and demands placed on me as a new wife and mother became extremely challenging. There were times when Gary's consistent mood swings transitioned him into someone who I didn't recognize. This was not the same man who I fell in love with and ultimately married.

If the expectations of our apartment being spotless were not met, there was a consequence. This criterion was measured by the use of a "white glove" examination by looking under beds for dust, wiping furniture with his hand to see if it was wiped clean, or checking window blinds for soil; if my response to him or his demands were not met to Gary's satisfaction, there were penalties. At a young age, I experienced being a victim of silence or passive aggressive behavior, abusive comments, or total alienation for a number of days as though we were not married.

I have today come to understand that passive-aggressive behavior correlates with retaliatory silence. I've also learned that negative attitudes can surface out of nowhere and be both frightening and discouraging. It became painfully clear that when one is victimized by verbal attacks through name-calling or acts of hostility, we never forget the words said, the body language, the time of day it was said, and the imprint it leaves on one's psyche. It was during this first year of marriage that I realized that I was now the wife of a demanding, sexist, and abusive husband.

Our New Home

When Myishia was seven years old and J.R. was two, we moved from the "Brown House" to our first real home in East Elmhurst. We lived there for about ten years. Many of the experiences of emotional, physical, and psychological abuse continued for each of us in the family, but this secret remained within the confines of our home. Some of these years, I have to say were filled with fun, excitement, and in many instances, contentment. We traveled as a family; enjoyed holidays together, shopped for new furniture together, and created an environment worthy of our living space. We felt that we were creating what most families want: a proud and bountiful life. I also have to say my mindset remained positive in hoping to give my children a worthwhile home life.

Nevertheless, there were more times of strife and confusion in our household than I care to remember. Many of my friends knew I was in a difficult relationship, as it was perceived that I had a "daddy" and not a husband. Gary was very controlling and wanted everything to go his way. If it did not go his way, there were consequences.

As the years passed, Gary's mood swings became more constant and unbearable. His periods of shifting from a sense of well-being moved to one of restlessness and peculiarity in moments. Unfortunately, these mood swings began to occur more frequently, disruptively, and unpredictably causing me to suspect emotionally something was wrong. These sporadic variations in temperament were demonstrated through silence, passivity, or indifference without explanation. He would then shift to aggressiveness through anger, resentment, and a strong need for control of his environment. During these frequent and unpredictable mood swings, we became victims in our own home.

However, most people, even our nucleus and extended family and friends, did not know the severity of Gary's mood swings. As an intimidated as well as loyal wife, I was very silent about the negative side of our relationship. Although he was very stern, obsessive-compulsive, and had consistent mood swings, out of devotion to my children, I remained in that relationship for nineteen years. Because of my upbringing, including the voids and fulfillment I experienced in my relationship with my mom and dad, I strongly believed in a two-parent household. Today, I recognize and acknowledge that not only did I unconsciously suffer, but so did both of my children.

The Violation of The Psychological Contract

Before marriage, I anticipated that my future husband would continue to care for me with kindness and respect. I anticipated that he would consistently provide for me with synergy, substance, and satisfaction in such a way that I would consistently feel safe and secure in the relationship; I also anticipated that these feelings of safety and security would be reciprocal throughout our bond. These were my thoughts and expectations; however, like so many others, I never shared these thoughts and feelings with the man I married. My faith, sprinkled with a cup of naiveté, led me to believe that this unspoken or unwritten contract of silent expectations would be honored. This unspoken expectation or psychological contract experienced in relationships is the basis of any relationship that is dynamic, rather than static. Will one of us violate this psychological contract? Now enlightened and more mature, if I had the chance, I would verbally seek answers to the following five questions:

1. Will we continue to communicate with each other in a respectful and loving way?
2. Will we participate in providing each other with a loving and tranquil household?
3. Will we be cognizant of the significance of our marital covenant by refraining from emotional, psychological or physical abuse?

4. Will my choice of a life-long partner live up to my visualization of the future as a principled, honorable, and a moral person… until death do we part?
5. How will we maintain a level of satisfaction that meets the unspoken expectations of our psychological contract?

Unfortunately, this contract was violated a number of times during my nineteen-year first marriage. As a mature adult, discerning the choices I needed to make in life turned out to be a complex task, especially in love and marriage. I frequently made choices based on how I saw myself which may not have been an accurate perception. Despite the increased knowledge about myself, as well as the lessons learned from the misguided selection of my first husband, combined with the mysterious emotion called love, I gained wisdom from this bad choice. At that time, I was influenced by my passion and immaturity, which preceded my logical decision-making tendencies.

On Becoming A Divorce Statistic

History dictates that many of us, when seeking love, seem to place more emphasis on the external façade of our life-partner's perspective rather than what's truly important in any relationship: unconditional love, trust, loyalty, respect, and synergy. Today, couples married for less than nineteen years have more than a fifty percent divorce rate in the United States. For people who have had multiple marriages, the rate is substantially higher. By me placing more emphasis on the aura of love and not its core value, nineteen years later, I too became a statistic through divorce.

Let me preface the following sentiments by stating that I believe in the sacrament of marriage and what it represents. In retrospect, my experiences and anticipation during my first marriage did not meet my expectations. Once the "honeymoon" was over, it wasn't long before my heart dropped! I was no longer my parent's little girl, but rather a wife and mother. The pre-marital romance and excitement of consistent dating, immature sex, and feeling valued through unconditional love, slowly sizzled away. The reality of my youth, immaturity, and impulsive decisions finally set in. Before I married for the second time, I had to know and learn more about me in order to *move out of my own way*.

The Life of a Single Mother

It was difficult being a single mother at that time in my life. Because I married as a teenager and not accustomed to dating, I learned very quickly that dating in the late 1970's was not for me. I was young, attractive, but naïve to the lively and free-spirited seventies. I realized that I preferred stability rather than experiencing the unknown.

During our year-long separation, Gary never gave up pursuing me; he was relentless. I finally agreed to try again at reestablishing our relationship and he ultimately moved in with us. He was my first love and I really knew no other life. Unfortunately, time proved that stripes do not change. After three years of perplexing hard work and consistent effort to make our marriage work, this turned out to be our last attempt. I finally divorced Gary in 1982 and began living as a single mother of a daughter in college and a teenage son at home with me. As a parent, this also was quite a ride as there were many adjustments to be made in each of our individual lives. Reestablishing a new identity was not only a novelty for me, but also difficult for J.R. to see his mother in such a different role. Once my children became adults and left home, I strongly felt the absence of their love. Feeling independent, but alone, I then waited for the void of their absence to be filled by the unknown.

Love is Not a Choice: It is a Psychological Need

"Do not be anxious about anything, but in everything, by prayer and petition, with thanksgiving, present your requests to God." Philippians 4:6

During discussions with my adult siblings, each of us, except the first born, my oldest brother, Malvane, revealed that we had low self-esteem. As a result of my own low self-esteem, I searched for love, thought I found it, grew from it, let it go, and sought it again. Aside from my baby brother, William, the closest memory of having this feeling where love was openly expressed was from the love of my son and daughter. Through their innocence, dependency, smiles, laughter, hugs, and excitement, whenever they had the urge, they spontaneously expressed their love for me.

I specifically recall one summer evening returning home from work on my last leg of public transportation, the bus line, I saw my two young children, ages six and eleven, waiting with anticipation and excitement to see their mother exit the bus. This was not a consistent habit by them, so I was pleasantly surprised. I cannot adequately explain the joy I felt in seeing their elated faces and adoration for me once I had both feet on the ground. They somehow knew what time I was expected, stopped their active play time in the neighborhood, and walked the two blocks to the bus stop to meet me. These are memorable experiences that made me recognize that love is not a choice, but rather a psychological need. Psychologically, my void to feel loved that day was filled by this unexpected occurrence.

Choice: What Motivated Me to Remarry?

"When you ask, you do not receive, because you ask with wrong motives, that you may spend what you get on your pleasures." James 4:3

Many years ago, while going through the divorce proceedings. I gave thought to whether I should remarry. As expressed earlier, the first time around was not at all what I expected it to be. What I decided to do was to seek a richer, more palatable, and clearer understanding of why I need this amorphous, immeasurable, subjective emotion called "love". I therefore approached it and responded to love in a more proactive and penetrating way.

There are those of us, who like me, when making the decision to remarry, ponder and reflect on the challenges of life. We have raised children, persevered obstacles, and, through introspection and self-awareness, had to learn to trust the process once again. Miraculously, once we find that "life partner" or "soul mate", we intentionally choose under this immeasurable emotion never to fall out of love with each other. This is considered to be a liberal choice that both parties in the relationship openly voice, honor, and commit to as one union.

Since we cannot change people, the acceptance of each other's differences is the cement that binds us.

Before remarrying, the major question I pondered was, "Why do we sometimes experience confusion and blunders in choosing a mate whom we eventually marry, separate from, and ultimately seek a divorce. Yet, we still have a desire to remarry?" I believe it is because as human beings, we long for companionship; someone we can trust to accept our differences, nurture our spirit, and continue to love us unconditionally.

Before validating love for the second time, I read and studied one of the greatest expressions of love that I've ever come across. It is from the Bible in First Corinthians 13:4-8 and unexpectedly recited by my sister Roberta at my wedding:

> *Love is patient and kind…with both people and wildlife;*
> *Love does not envy or boast…it doesn't sing one's own praises but rather boasts about others good work and gives God the Glory and all the credit;*
> *Love is not arrogant or rude…it does not hold over people one's status, power, influence, or knowledge;*
> *Love isn't rude…but rather polite displaying protocols and proper politeness;*
> *Love does not insist on its own way…but gives priority and precedence to others, even if it has to compromise;*
> *Love does not rejoice with wrongdoing, but rejoices with the truth…it never delights in other people's sins…instead, it rejoices in the truth of the Bible;*
> *Love bears all things…yes…the absolute word "all"… hopes all things…hopes for the best for all concerned, endures all*

things…all, like being, abused, disrespected, and mistreated, and so on.

These written verses in First Corinthians are God's way of helping me and you to understand this multifaceted, yet humble, emotion called "love". It is meaningful to me because I plan to be in this sacrament of marriage for the long haul, bearing all things.

I now have an awareness of how my life can be fulfilled with the balance that God had in mind for me when it was said in Ephesians 4:2-3: "Be completely humble and gentle; be patient, bearing with one another in love. Make every effort to keep the unity of the Spirit through the bond of peace."

Finding Myself

When in the throes of love, and in instances when it was abused as it was in my first marriage, it is not an emotion that I can demand to surface again at will. Because I was ill-treated, love is not an emotion that I can command to act or respond instantly. And when love is not nurtured, it is **not** an emotion that I can have dominion over because I feel powerful in the moment. Therefore, for a while, I resisted love from taking over my life. I had to learn to find myself to *move out of my own way*.

I took this journey with the recognition that in order to be successful in the choices I make, including remarrying, I must commit myself to do the following:

Seek Self-Knowledge

First and foremost, in seeking love, I needed to love myself. I had to re-evaluate my values, beliefs, and principles that involuntarily drive my daily behavior. Are these instilled, but instinctively driven beliefs, values, and principles, a positive force in my life, or barriers to growth? If it is a positive force, will I live a life with a positive attitude toward my existence and everything in it? If they become barriers, will I have negative attitudes toward life and everything in it? Am I in denial about who I *think* I am or have I courageously evaluated myself by accepting authentic feedback? It is also essential that I reflect on my *God-given* gifts in order for them to be cultivated and that I introspect on my shortcomings in order to self-correct. My spiritual and intellectual growth is part of God's will. Therefore, I had to answer the following two questions before I could go to the next phase in reaffirming my prospective mate:

1. What are three strengths that I know about me?
2. What are three weaknesses that I know about me?

Visualization:

When Seeking love, it will necessitate me to have at least a realistic visualization of my prospective *"soul mate"*. This is the person who I will spend the balance of my life with. Therefore, more introspection was required by asking myself the following:

1. Will the person I am looking for be aligned with my values, beliefs, and principles?
2. Will the person I am looking for support my talents and gifts and balance my shortcomings?
3. Will the person that I am looking for share my Christian views and be equally yoked?

4. As I journey through the maturation process, with whom do I envision in my life to be the devoted friend, loyal companion, and dedicated spouse until death do we part.
5. Will he help me to grow and allow me to help him to grow? If so, this sounds like my soul mate.

Finding My Soul Mate

"We know that in all things God works for the good of those who love Him". Romans 8:28

Part of the mystery of finding true love is that love has its own mind! During the 1980's, life was rapidly changing from the idealistic dreams of the sixties to the new conservatism in social, economic and political life, characterized by the policies of President Ronald Reagan. This was the decade of an explosion of blockbuster movies, and the emergence of cable networks like MTV, which launched the careers of many iconic artists. The 1980's were definitely exciting times! It was also the era of the rise of the young, urban, professionals called "Yuppies". They were known to be ambitious and well-educated city dwellers that had a professional career and lifestyle.

It was a difficult time for me. So many things in my life were happening simultaneously. All of my life I lived in the suburbs in a one, two, or three-story house. As a result of my divorce, I was now living in a twenty-four story high rise in an urban environment. I also, for the first time, was raising my two children alone with one income. Additionally, I was in graduate school, working toward my master's degree. Life was different, but exciting. I was not looking for love, but rather a life of independence.

I met my soul mate, Roland, in August 1983. I was divorced for about twelve months at that time. By today's standards, I can consider myself blessed or cursed. I married my first love as a teenager, lacking time to know life as a young adult and meeting my second love in less than two years of experiencing the single life. The positive side is that I found my soul mate; the negative side was the uncertainty. "How did I know for sure?" "Did I explore all my options?"

I was with a girlfriend at a wildly popular social club called "Leviticus" in downtown Manhattan when I first saw my "soul mate" that I would describe as a Yuppie. Actually, it was my girlfriend, Louise, who first noticed him and brought him to my attention. She was more interested than I was as he looked like a "heartbreaker" to me. By my standards, he was tall, dark, and handsome, with a lean body that said he cared about his appearance. He was impressive because of his six foot four-inch stature that also stood out amongst many as he was dramatically dressed in all black. He had an attractive black beard and a heavy mustache similar to that of Teddy Pendergrass. Based on the trend of the era, I recall that his shirt was provocatively and stylishly unbuttoned to show off his fourteen-inch gold chain, lying prominently in the middle of his muscular chest.

However, upon leaving a few hours later, his best friend, Pedro, who revealed many years later that he thought I was a good match, introduced us. At that moment, my back was to Roland, so I wasn't sure who his mysterious friend was.

Although I was not interested in a relationship, when I turned around to see who he wanted me to meet, I was surprised that it was the same "heartbreaker" that Louise and I had spoken about earlier. When we were introduced, what I immediately noticed about him was his benevolent soul which was transparent through the windows of his eyes. He had on a Gucci watch, showed me a timid smile, and spoke in a very deep voice. Contrary to his playboy image, he was quiet, reserved, and appeared to be conventional. We danced once, chatted a bit about who we were, exchanged phone numbers through the trend of business cards, and finally said goodnight. Since I didn't hear from him over the next few weeks, I removed his image from my psyche, giving him no further thought.

      About a month later, I was planning to meet my girlfriends at the same club. Upon entering the lounge area where we agreed to meet, who did I see but Roland! He was sitting alone in his business attire looking very professional, but pensive. His back was to me, so I assertively tapped him on the shoulder. He immediately turned, looked at me with surprise, stood, put his arms around me and said, "Where have you been? I lost your number, but I thought you would call me". That was the beginning of our relationship. On a superficial level, I came to learn that he had a beautiful black car, a conservative frame of mind, and knew how to respectfully treat a woman. On a deeper level, however, he eventually revealed to me that he was rebounding from a previously severed relationship that had hurt him deeply. It was during these intimate discussions that I discovered how passionate he was about family, friends, and relationships. Unbeknownst to me, I became the mystical and therapeutic remedy needed for Roland to approach a new chapter in his life and he became my joy.

The Canoeing Incident
or
What the First Year of Marriage Must Be Like

During the first year of our relationship, on one of our many adventurous weekend dates, we decided to do something unique by going canoeing. We started out early in the morning with two other couples, Bobby and Marilyn and Josh and Savannah. What a beautiful day it was! The blue and cloudless sky was tranquilly veiled above us, and the bright and shining sun was radiating its warmth. However, contrary to what seemed like a perfect day, the water appeared to be somewhat rough, choppy, dark and unsettled.

Nonetheless, after spending some time on land talking and laughing together, each couple decided to take the risk and navigate separate canoes. We therefore proceeded to cheerfully step into an unsecure and chancy vessel as none of us had ever experienced this type of irregular water-adventure before now. Conversely, although new in our relationship, I felt safe and secure with my prospective "soul mate". I felt confident that it would be a fun and exciting adventure. Well, was I mistaken! What I did not do was anticipate our personality differences under challenging situations. We both had an individualized need for control of our circumstances; we both had a need to demonstrate our personal power in order to win; we both had a desire to pilot the canoe as we saw fit! After about a half-hour of calmly posing our respective directives, opinions, and commands, we were literally going around in circles for what seemed like miles and miles ending up experiencing a no-win situation while still in rough and turbulent water. During the next hour, we finally began to realize that we were in a major communicative conflict, as well as in a dangerous situation. During this unforgettable hour, we eventually began to raise our voices, attempting to steer one way while the other wanted to go another! We kept going around and around, actually in circles, but never traveling in a direction of safety. In my mind, I felt like we were "white-water rafting" even though we were simply in a canoe with two stubborn individuals at the helm.

For the entire run, this "canoeing incident" caused us to become exhausted and worn out, feel frightened and anxious, and become cynical and distrustful of each other. We both thought the canoe would overturn, or worse, we would ultimately drown. Close to the end of this horrific ordeal, as we got closer to shore, I was almost in tears as Roland stepped out of the boat and proceeded to walk the short distance in the shallow water to shore. While he was traipsing through the water, he ran into Josh who also abandoned his "girl". After a brief discussion with Josh, Roland realized that Josh and Savannah had a parallel episode that we were thoroughly familiar with.

What I Learned

What I learned from this "canoeing incident" is that we can only have one leader in a relationship. When we don't trust who is leading, guiding, or simply supporting us as needed, we are threatening the success of the relationship! When we don't do the inner work necessary to consciously seek to know who we truly are as well as who our mate is, accepting our similarities as well as our differences, we compromise the benefit of each other's strengths, which ultimately will balance our limitations. Through this compromise of "respect" for each other's uniqueness, we enhance our level of safety and security, peace and joy in our home life, as well as comfort in our own skin!

Of course, over the next three decades, we laughed about the "Canoeing Incident" many times. Sometimes we even use it to help counsel others in their relationships. This analogy is similar to what the first years of marriage can be like for newlyweds. In ending this anecdote, below are two substantive marital lessons we learned on that dreadful but impactful day four years prior to our marriage. Each lesson revolves around the necessary inner work needed to maintain a marriage or relationship:

1. First and foremost, it is essential that we recognize and accept that only one of us can lead. Therefore, we must constantly <u>work together</u> to accept this during episodic phases in our relationship. This will prevent us from facing the unnecessary challenge of leading our family in the wrong direction, especially during a crisis.

2. If we are going to have a meaningful, fulfilling, and loving relationship in our marriage or partnership, we must <u>work hard</u> to respect each other's similarities (sometimes this works against us), as well as our differences (we sometimes want them to be just like us).

> In most instances, we gravitate to our opposites for the unconscious purpose of making us whole and balanced!

While introspecting down memory lane, the manifestations that occurred for me to become unstuck took place time and time again. My tumultuous journey to find love was like a roller coaster filled with excitement, unexpected twists and turns, hard and sudden stops and surprise endings! Yet, I was able to find my soul mate.

Evaluating My Choice

Be wise about what is good, and innocent about what is evil.
Romans 16:19

As Roland and I continued to see each other, it was the beginning of a pretty rapid, quixotic dating expedition. After getting to know him better, including his quirks, love for beer, and adventurous spirit, I discovered that he was intelligent; he was also a logical thinker, college educated, and had a professional job as a manager in the world of work. These qualities were important to me as they were the opposite of the characteristics of my first husband. What was really amazing about him was that he came with no baggage…no wife, no previous wife, no children, and no criminal record!

Not only did he impress me with our lengthy and intimate conversations about our beliefs, principles and values, although there were many differences, we appeared to have shared much in common regarding life in general. I also discovered that he was very connected to Our Lord, Jesus Christ, through his life-long involvement with his church. On our very first Saturday night date, contrary to typical weekend behavior in New York City, we ended our date relatively early, around midnight. I was impressed with his value of loyalty as he was committed to his duties as a Trustee at the church he attended. We appeared to be equally yoked, synergized, and the prospective "soul mates" for each other. As we continued to see each other, I kept looking for some flaw, but other than our age difference, I couldn't find any. While dating, we saw each other every weekend, fell in love, travelled together, and began to create our love nest.

After my son left home to be on his own, for economic reasons and our desire to be with each other as much as possible, Roland and I eventually made the choice to cohabitate. Furthermore, after my unsuccessful relationship in my first marriage, my safety choice was to experience a live-in relationship.

As an empty nester, this part of my life was adventurous, fun-filled, romantic, and very exciting. I was still relatively young, single, independent, and madly in love with this man and his zest for life. We were seldom seen without the other, constantly on the go, and eventually became known to be an "item" followed by the sentiment, "Roland loves him some Carole."

The "Pursuit Strategy"

To all who were in our presence, it was obvious we were madly, passionately, and unmistakably in love. We were perceived as a couple who were very busy, yet content with the status quo as we both had great professional careers, romance, and much joy in our lives. I felt that I had found my soul mate! Although he was younger than I, we envisioned no problems that we could not overcome as long as we had God in our lives and each other. We felt that we knew each other well, respected each other's differences, space, opinions, and idiosyncrasies. We were equally yoked, felt safe and secure with or without the presence of the other, valued trust in each other, lived in contentment, and appeared to be the ideal couple.

Remember when I said earlier that the first time I experienced the emotion of love was in recognizing the love of my youngest brother, William. I also indicated that the second time I felt true love was as a mother of my children, Myishia and J.R. The third time, my inherent need to be loved was fulfilled by this new man in my life, Roland. Although I was not looking for fostering another relationship, not yet anyway, God had other plans for me.

As time moved on, Roland wanted more. Earlier in our relationship, he had made a conscious decision that he wanted to get married and that I was his choice. However, he didn't share this with me at that time. Actually, it was another three years before our love was tested to the standard of a life-long commitment. He did state that he doesn't believe in divorce, meaning when he does marry, he is in it for the long haul. He subsequently and confidentially developed a "pursuit strategy" to ensure I would ultimately become his wife. Being as content as we were, this was an agenda of which I was unaware.

My Mother's Wisdom and Influence

Roland's character and personality were unique to me and very much filled with the unknown. However, when I pondered the choice to take the risk of moving into a relationship for the second time to marry Roland, I sought the wisdom of my mother. In speaking to my mother about this significant crossroad in my life, her response is what inspired me. She simply said, "When you find true love, which doesn't come often, you have to grab it because it is hard to find again!" This was the clincher for me. Her advice fulfilled my need to feel loved and belonged.

What I knew for sure was that the probability of success in any relationship results from understanding and accepting that this progression involves ingredients such as trust, open-mindedness, and introspection on both sides. This option to remarry was the beginning of the creation of a life worth living.

The Surprise

We both were of the mindset that something as trivial as age was not a factor in the lives of adults. He was very cavalier about it and so was I. There were just too many real issues to worry about in today's society other than age. I knew he was younger than I was; he knew that I was older than him; he was aware that I was previously married, divorced, and had two children. I definitely came with baggage! He came with none except his heavy secret: the exact number of years in our age difference. In many of our intimate discussions, Roland spoke to the fact that he never dated anyone younger than he was.

Even while in high school and college, he was always attracted to older women. I happened to be one of them.

After being in relationship with Roland for more than three years, I vividly remember his proposal, which I almost turned down. It was not because I did not love him or want him for my lifelong partner, but rather the fear of the legalities associated with an unknown conduit of the future. Therefore, I cautiously responded to the proposal with the question, "Why change what we currently have?" I was very serious. I was concerned that marriage would interfere with or ruin the love and respect that we currently had for each other. Roland was loyal, passionate, responsible, disciplined, conscientious, ethical, respectful, and fun to be around. I felt that I had to make a <u>*choice*</u> to remain as we were, cohabitating, or take the risk of making our relationship legal and manage all that comes with lawful situations. For example, as we mature, will our age difference affect our relationship? Since I knew that the national divorce rate was well over fifty percent, I did not want to go through the agony of another divorce. He knew how I felt about marriage, so it came as quite a surprise to find out his actual age when we finally went for the marriage license.

Overcoming the Act of Betrayal

Once we were at the license bureau in preparation for our wedding day in May, I was livid after hearing Roland's well-kept secret. For the first time in our relationship, he revealed to me our decade age difference. I was shocked, as I thought perhaps he was five to six years younger than me, but I never thought it was by a decade. I felt that Roland had violated a major trust issue; he had maintained undisclosed and significant information about himself that was important to me and our relationship.

In his defense, Roland was focused. He immediately revealed to me in a genuine, apologetic, and regretful tone his "pursuit strategy". He didn't want to take the risk of losing me by telling me the differences in our age while we were still cohabitating. In that moment of doubt and betrayal, I imagined so many complications ahead of us because of this major time of life difference. For the next hour, as we waited to be called to get our license, I began to reflect on our four-year long relationship that caused me to fall in love with him.

An Hour of Reflection

I was truly hurt by this new information that Roland chose to share with me six weeks before we were to marry. I was not hurt because of the age gap, but rather by the breach of trust. What else will he breach? The wedding invitations were sent out, pre-marriage counseling accomplished, and the church and reception booked.

For four exciting years, we intimately grew to know and love each other. Roland's ability to express and demonstrate his love, passion for life and adventure were evident and consistent. I believe the measure of his love was actualized in 1985 when he demonstrated his most significant contribution to our relationship…loyalty. This was the year that his unconditional love for me was tested during a significant physical setback in my life.

Three years after meeting Roland, I was diagnosed with a herniated disc due to a work related injury and had to stay in a prone position for a total of six weeks. During this time, Roland was forever by my side. He fed me, bathed me, carried me to the bathroom, and kept me company without hesitation. Once the six weeks were up, it was determined that surgery, a laminectomy, was the only option left which required more psychological, emotional and physical support. Roland never wavered. In essence, for about a year, not only were we celibate, but also deprived of our normal adventurous and romantic date nights. His loyalty to me, his family, and his church is an amazing attribute that I thoroughly respected then and still do today. It took about an hour for me to readjust my thinking and emotions. In retrospect, he was probably right; I may have held off marrying him if he had revealed his secret during that time of my life in the eighties.

Therefore, after much thought about our love and our journey, I forgave Roland. We married on May 2nd, 1987, under the eyes and ears of one hundred witnesses. We went on an unforgettable two-week honeymoon and the rest is history! Today, after thirty years of marriage, there is no reason to elaborate on this moot point. I'm simply pleased that I had enough sense to *move out of my own way,* forgive him for his "Pursuit Strategy" and accepted Roland's sincere apology. My mother was right! You only find true love once!

My "Cougar" Status

Today, I realize that the age difference could have become a problem, if I had not shifted my thinking and *moved out of my own way*. I did this by not getting caught up with the stigma of ageism associated with the May-December relationship syndrome of the eighties. Of course, as friends and families on both sides met and appraised us, we both knew they had their opinions and sidebars about our age difference. In our dialogue about their perceptions, we both agreed that it didn't matter because they were not the ones in the relationship…we were. Actually, I enjoyed and still enjoy every minute of our stigmatized union. Roland was and still is a load of fun, an enigma in the eyes of some, misjudged by many, but ultimately he became a valued member of my family unit.

Without Trust, There is No Relationship

For I know the plans I have for you, "Declares the Lord", plans to prosper you and not to harm you, plans to give you hope and a future." Jeremiah 29:11

What is trust? Trust draws a parallel to conviction, passion, and confidence in whom or what I believe. In actuality, it is the "psychological contract" mentioned earlier that revolves around faith and feelings of assurance that *all* expectations of the other will be fulfilled, honored, and satisfied. When I remarried, I moved into a relationship with unspoken expectations that I would require to be treated similar to how I was treated during the dating or engagement stage. I have unspoken expectations that I will be treated with respect and admiration at all times.

My goal in this relationship is to be more aware of who I am, to assess my unspoken expectations, and to evaluate my balance, my Yin and Yang, between my "soul-mate" and me.

"In Chinese culture, Yin and Yang represent the two opposite principles in nature. Yin characterizes the feminine or negative nature of things and yang stands for the masculine or positive side. Yin and yang are in pairs, such as the moon and the sun, female and male, dark and bright, cold and hot, passive and active, etc. But yin and yang are not static or just two separated things. The nature of yin and yang lies in interchange and interplay of the two components. The alternation of day and night is such an example."

Personally, I've always appreciated the concept of Yin and Yang. Its philosophy has not only enhanced my self-worth, but also added to my creation of a life worth living, specifically in making a decision to remarry. This level of understanding has actually helped me shift my thinking to *move out of my own way*, remarry, and step into the unknown with love and confidence. Today, even with life's ups and downs, my husband and I are separate individuals, but united as one!

The Law of Attraction

Like Yin and Yang, Roland and I are very different. Actually, we are polarized in how we felt about our upbringing, our values, our personality types, and ourselves. I am an introvert and he is an extrovert; I am reserved while he is a free-spirit; I am an intellect while he is more emotional; I am detail-oriented while he is intuitive; I am an auditory learner while he is a visual learner; I was indoctrinated to religion as a mediocre catholic while he was nurtured as a devout Baptist; I am the middle child of five and he is the youngest of four; I was raised with both of my parents in my life while he barely knew his dad. I was raised in the tree-lined streets of the suburbs while he was raised in the "concrete jungle" in an urban community. I had a childhood where I considered the community and neighborhood to be relatively safe and non-threatening, while his childhood was filled with concerns of peer pressure, street gangs, and violence.

My most important value that I unconsciously live out today as an adult is to treat people according to how I want to be treated. Roland was raised in the church and comes from a family of Pastors and ministers. Therefore, his instilled value is to turn to the church when in need and to maintain a personal relationship with God. Nonetheless, even with our differences, we became one. For the first time in my adult life, I truly know what it feels like to be valued, loved, and adored by another adult in a marital relationship.

The Sacrament of Marriage

As a child in a woman's body, I perceived "LOVE" to be a euphoric and romantic place that we all, at some time or another, desire to seek and caress. As a mother and child bride, I understood the concept of unconditional love, but as a woman, I came to recognize that love is a capricious and emotional state of mind. I did all that I was taught to do to be considered a good wife the first time around. I revered my position as wife and mother but ultimately transitioned into the subservient and submissive spouse of the 1960s. Even by today's standards, being obedient and subservient is acceptable behavior in many marriages, including same-gender loving relationships. However, many of us have been taught by the social order or past generations in authority to be obedient without thought or reflection.

This behavior is evident and exposed when respect for the compliant spouse is obviously compromised through betrayal, emotional, psychological, or physical abuse. Of course, the success in any relationship is probable. I consider travelling through what I call "The Tunnel of Love and Marriage" a prerequisite to ensuring marriage success. It's not always going to be as bright as it is when going in. It is at the "Halfway" point when our marriage is truly tested. However, on coming out on the other side, we should be more mature, wiser, and at peace with each other, solidifying our love.

So, what is this "Tunnel of Love and Marriage"? In order to come out at the end…albeit more mature, wiser, and complete…yet still in love, requires that we use our imagination to take a look at what's inside.

Navigating the Tunnel of Love and Marriage: The Entrance

"Don't let anyone look down on you because you are young, but set an example for the believers in speech, in life, in faith and in purity." Timothy 4:12

In 1987, entering into or treading into the "Tunnel of Love and Marriage" with Roland for the first time was relatively risk-free since it is illuminated by the "light" from the mouth of the tunnel or by the outside of the entrance. The feeling of euphoria experienced at the entrance point is amazing.

During the first fifteen years of my marriage, Roland was with me every step of the way, causing me to consistently be in the "now"; feeling secure, exhilarated, and unafraid. However, as years passed and we proceeded through the "Tunnel", the light gradually began to dim, preventing me from being as optimistic as I was initially. Life got in the way. There were issues associated with finances, employment, rejection, crushed dreams, and self-esteem.

I missed the feeling of being in the "now", where I felt secure holding Roland's hand from day to day. The tunnel's initial light had a glow bright enough with which I could still look back and see the mouth of the entrance, but as I looked ahead, it required groping around to find my way. It was difficult for me to know what was in front of me when I couldn't see ahead. All I could do was trust the process. As I travelled further into the "Tunnel of Love and Marriage", the walls become closer, and the probing became more pronounced. It was not until I realized that I still had Roland's hand in mine, leading me, guiding me, supporting me, that I held his hand tighter and began to relax.

"The Halfway Point"

During my journey toward the halfway point, I had to think about the past two decades of our relationship, our current status as a couple, and how our future will transcend our existing struggles. Should I continue to hold on to the hand of my "soul mate" when I was uncertain about what lies ahead? I don't believe we are any different from other couples that have been married longer than a number of decades. When I questioned a few couples that celebrated their 50th anniversary, they shared stories similar to my experiences. As they passed the halfway point in the "Tunnel of Love and Marriage ", they had a choice to deliberately let go of their *"chosen one's"* hand or hold on tighter. Under either choice, they began to touch, explore, and discover the unknown boundaries of undisclosed life encounters.

While within the midpoint of the "Tunnel of Love and Marriage", Roland and I constantly turned around to see how far we had come, as we could no longer see the light at the beginning of the "Tunnel". When together we looked ahead of us, we still could not see how far we had to go to the end. This was unnerving as we thought there was no light to guide us, not understanding that God's light was always there.

At this point in the "Tunnel", we are now exploring crannies or *mood swings*, crevices, which are the same as *disappointments*, hearing unusual periods of silence, like stillness versus laughter, encountering unknown species, as with unexpected shifts in personalities, and experiencing anxiety and fear, like aging, or illness, which gradually or suddenly appears. The key to our marital success is continuously holding on to each other's hand, especially while going through the halfway mark of the "Tunnel of Love and Marriage."

As we continued along our uncertain journey through the maze of the tunnel, there were so many challenges Roland and I faced causing us to reevaluate the love we had, how it had been challenged, and how it could be reignited. Our life experiences as a couple included educational pursuits, career failures and successes, new jobs, as well as job losses, fluctuating finances, family transitions, relocation, and the awareness or lack of awareness in our individual psychological, emotional, and spiritual growth.

As we passed the halfway point in the "Tunnel of Love and Marriage", I now had a choice to introspect on my individualized needs which could cause me to deliberately let go of my partner's hand or to hold on tighter. Under either choice, my spouse and I would have to continue to touch, explore, and discover the unknown dark boundaries while moving towards the end of the "Tunnel of Love and Marriage".

During the difficult times of the economic downturn, Roland recognized that I needed him emotionally. I was falling apart under the stress and strain of concern. He subsequently evaluated his life and being equally yoked, made a conscious choice to diligently respond to God's calling. He knowingly *moved out of his own way* by giving up past destructive behaviors, prostrating himself before God, asking for forgiveness for his old actions.

While in college, Roland was introduced to the taste of alcohol, especially beer. He ultimately mistreated his mind and body through over-indulgence of this substance later in life. He humbly requested from God a new life. He asked God to remove the desire for the taste of alcohol or beer from his pallet. God listened and immediately responded by creating the pathway to spiritual change. Since then, Roland has never touched alcohol again.

For two years, Roland, together with other members of our church, consistently attended weekly sessions under our pastor's leadership. Roland's goal was to learn God's word and become a servant as an ordained deacon. Ultimately, in 2010, Roland was ordained as a Deacon at our church, Victory for the World Church, located in Stone Mountain, Georgia. For three years after this ordination, I no longer knew Roland. This transition changed his personality to one of sternness and control. Since Roland's installation, he has transitioned into a totally different person since he abstained from indulging in any kind of alcoholic beverage, including his favorite, which was beer. If you recall, I only knew this fun-loving, passionate man under this influence. He then became a stranger to me. Yet, I did not let go of his hand.

Today, however, he is back as the fun-loving Roland I fell in love with. He is at peace with his destiny to be a Deacon and feels fulfilled. He also met the long-standing predictions by his family that this position as a Deacon or Minister was his calling. Today, Roland proudly and with honor leads the Security Team and is the Armor Bearer for the Pastor and esteemed guests.

As I travel forward, I have become less frightened by the unknown and less inclined to let go of Roland's hand. I knew this desire to maintain a relationship with Roland superseded my fear to turn around. Although it is still too dark in the tunnel to see the "light" at the end, and secure ground, God's guidance inspired me to trust in Him and His direction. I keep in my heart "For I have plans for you, declares the Lord, plans to prosper you and not to harm you; plans to give you hope and a future." Jeremiah 29:11

After passing this midpoint, the tunnel became more familiar. I had become accustomed to the crannies, the crevices, the unusual periods of silence, the unknown species, and experiencing anxiety and fear. However, although there were other times that I felt like I weathered the unknown alone, there were times when the desire, hunger, and thirst for my husband's hand shifted from dependency to independence. Not only did we begin to respect each other's need for space, but we also acknowledged our differences and the inherent need for control that each of us has as human beings.

Today, as an adult-adult union, we make every effort to respect each other's needs and desires so that we no longer depend on each other to the same extent as we did in the past to find our way. Yet, this is only the halfway point.

The End of the Tunnel

"Let all that you do be done in love." 1 Corinthians 16:14

I am now past the midpoint of the "Tunnel", very slowly and independently finding my way. During this journey in the "Tunnel", months, weeks, and many years have gone by while still working on finding my way to a place of love and self-respect. This level of anticipation is constantly there while I am creating a life worth living.

Subsequently, by *moving out of my own way*, I began to thrive as a woman, but in a different way. Recognizing and acknowledging that relationships can be a power struggle, I learned to acquiesce as needed in the interest of reverence. My soul mate and I both needed to determine how to walk in our own brand of dignity and still relate to the other. We both needed to feel respected for who we are and what we bring to the relationship. Through this level of awareness, my prayer is that when we exit the "Tunnel of Love and Marriage" together, still holding hands, our relationship as husband and wife will still be rooted in trust, friendship, respect and loyalty. We will look back and honor our journey, knowing that we have weathered the storm together.

In conclusion, from my vantage point and experience as a first and second-time married woman, my old and new relationships have encouraged and necessitated me to rediscover who I am. This assessment could be beneficial to me or detrimental to my well-being, contingent upon my honest and candid self-analysis. In other words, I may need to self-correct. If successful, it will satisfy my need to feel content with my spouse even when his need for control overpowers my need. If not successful in molding myself according to my needs, perhaps I will again go through the lengthy and laborious process of *"moving out of my own way"*. I will finally accept and validate that I am truly the person who Roland encountered, was enamored by, and ultimately became his spouse for life. The prerequisite to being at this place of wonderment is honestly evaluating what it was like going through the "Tunnel of Love and Marriage".

Through the intimate lenses of a loving partner, Roland helped me in this process. He gazed, assessed, analyzed, revamped as needed, and in some instances attempted to change whom he would like me to be. Of course, I did the same to him. In the end, we both agree that our selection of each other as spouses have met each other's expectations to love and trust each other until death do we part. We are definitely soul mates.

Feeling Mature in My Second Marriage

Contrary to my first marriage, I am in a rich reciprocal relationship with my current husband, where mutual expectations and life choices are discussed and respected; I learned to be confident, self-assured, and trusting. In summary, although there were some disappointments along life's expedition in both marriages, I learned three things:

1. To appreciate that overcoming obstacles, as painful as it may be, builds character. I was being prepared to listen for God's cues for the next door that was about to be opened.
2. To evaluate and measure life's challenges as sweet results by assessing my current triumphs, victories, and accomplishments.
3. To maintain humility, gratitude, and faith in God's blessings as no one but God knows what tomorrow will bring. He is the only one who knows how the story will end.

Choice: I Married my "Soul Mate" and Rightfully So!

"We know that in all things God works for the good of those who love Him." Romans 8:28

Feeling valued has everything to do with one's self esteem. Prior to meeting Roland, no one had ever called me "Baby Doll" or "Uno Number One". With the exception of this new man in my life, no one had ever kissed me on my forehead while holding me in his arms as a way of expressing his love for me. No man had ever demonstrated his non-sexual desire for me through obvious excitement when he spotted me on the crowded streets of New York City; no one ever literally

<u>ran</u> up to me, lifted me up in the air, swung me around, hugged and kissed me like I was the last person on earth.

These behaviors of passion I saw in the movies, but never in life. It was these small, yet huge, gestures, these combined words and actions that for once in my life caused me to feel complete! That was thirty-four years ago and I am still loved by this man, my current husband, who receives the same love in return. He still makes my heart beat faster when I hear his voice, see his smile, or simply be in his presence.

However, we are the fortunate ones! Today, people divorce at the drop of a hat! It is almost predictable how long the newly married couple will stay together. It is of my opinion that our need for love is so great that many of our choices are made in the blind. Until we pass through the painful process of learning more about ourselves by consistently assessing who we truly are, identifying and owning our strengths as well as weaknesses, and clarifying our values, principles, and beliefs, we will continue to choose those who we think will meet our "love" needs. Although love is free and sometimes hits us like a shooting star from the sky, knowing ourselves precludes the importance of knowing our marriage partner as well.

Through my current marriage of thirty years, established during a more mature age, I've come to understand that love and marriage are balanced with rich universal ingredients of combined patience, tenderness, understanding, perseverance, and, most importantly, acceptance and respect for our differences. During this transition, **real** love grows with faith, trust, and belief in each other and, more importantly, in each other's dreams. This level of trust and understanding will make each of us whole by virtue of our interactions. Love is really the desire to be understood and to understand your mate. It stands to reason that I cannot *truly love* that which I don't understand… however, when I accepted what each of us bring to the table in that understanding, I actually became one with whom I fell in love. Trust has everything to do with its success.

What a joy it is when we know ourselves well enough to practice love in this way, with this mindset, and with this attitude toward love and relationships. I have embraced the fact that every child needs love, as love makes us feel whole, appreciated, secure and validated as human beings.

So what makes being in love so influential, powerful, and commanding? One particular reason for this magnificent stimulus and control is because love is not something we can live *without* except by being deceased, even while we appear to be alive. According to Mother Teresa, *"The hunger for love is much more difficult to remove than the hunger for bread"*.

> **We must realize that**
>
> **our future lies chiefly**
>
> **in our own hands.**
>
> Paul Robeson

Lesson Four
"The Use of My Most Precious Gift: The Freedom of Choice"

"As human beings, the crown of God's creation, God has "set eternity in the hearts of people" Ecclesiastes 3:11

  This fourth lesson on "The Use of My Most Precious Gift: The Freedom of Choice" is really about my inherent need for control. It is a thoughtful and reflective lesson on the choices I have made to undo mistakes in order to turn my life around. This precious gift of the freedom of choice was in many instances in my life transformed into a consequence rather than a benefit. Even though I unconsciously knew that God granted me the gift of free choice, in many instances I still abused it. In practical terms, I mistreated my most precious gift by taking it for granted.

  How many times have I made a decision or made a choice without thinking about the consequence of that choice? How many times, even after serious thought, have I made a choice and wished I had chosen another path? How many times have I regretted the choice I made and did not learn anything from the experience? While travelling down memory lane, I revisited the number of times I made a spontaneous decision because of my need to be in control of an outcome, right or wrong.

The Impact Birth Order Had on My Freedom of Choice

"Consider it pure joy, my brother, whenever you face trials of many kinds, because you know that the testing of your faith develops perseverance."
James 1:2-3

My brother Malvane is four years older than I; my sister Roberta is two years older. Accustomed to being in their shadow, I unconsciously looked up to both of them without thinking about "the freedom of choice". When I was fourteen months old, my sister Olivia was born. Six years later, my mother gave birth to my brother William who was the last to join us in the sibling hierarchy.

Due to my birth order, I became known as the "mysterious' middle child of five. According to a published study on "Birth Order" by Jeffrey Klugger, and reported in 2007 by Dan Cray in Time Magazine, *"Of all things that shape who we are, few seem more arbitrary than the sequence in which we and our siblings pop out of the womb. Maybe it's your genes that make you a gifted athlete, your training that makes you an accomplished actress, an accident of brain therapy that makes you a drunk instead of a president. But in family after family, case study after case study, the simple roll of the birth-date dice has an odd and arbitrary power of its own."*

The Middle Child Syndrome

As a middle child, I had issues that definitely took on "an odd and arbitrary power of its own". My memory travels back to days as a toddler where I unconsciously chose to exercise my spiritual right of free choice by following my mother everywhere. If she went into the bathroom, kitchen, bedroom, I was right behind her. My most vivid memories of my childhood is of my mother standing by the stove cooking; I can still see my small frame standing next to her, holding on to her nightgown, with my two middle fingers in my mouth. I was probably similar to a well-trained puppy that cannot speak, but adores its master. However, my compliant behaviors shifted by age two. I now became my mother's worse nightmare as I transformed into an angry and unruly toddler.

The Root of My Anger

Years later, I discovered that my mother breastfed all of her children, except me. As I understand it, my mother developed pneumonia immediately after my birth, which prevented my breastfeeding cycle to begin. I was further awakened to how this experience may have shaped my personality by researching the psychological benefits of breastfeeding.

By interpreting recent research, a child who is breastfed is offered a sense of continuity from pre-to-post birth life. The consistent physical closeness of their mother is comforting and soothing for the fetus, until the newborn is released from the close, dark womb into an overwhelming experience of bright lights, loud noises, and new odors or smells. The need at this pivotal point in the world of the living is essential to their emotional health.

Consequently, as an adult, through exercising my spiritual right of free choice, I chose to explore and understand the cause or root of my emotional and confusing behavior. I sought out and became aware that some of my issues were caused by feelings of abandonment as a child. Apparently, a few things happened. What I missed during my infant years by not being breastfed was the secure gaze of my mother's eyes and warmth of her body. Because of this void, it took years for me to emotionally understand that I was loved, protected, and secure in my environment. It took decades before I understood and was able to wrap my brain around the fact that my mother was always there to provide for my needs for the rest of my dependent years. Needless to say, this level of understanding was a gradual process, not resonating for me until I was well into my adult years.

In the Time magazine article, Dan Cray stated, "Stuck for life in a center seat, middle children get shortchanged even on family resources. Unlike the firstborn, who spends at least some time as the only child eldest, and the last born who hangs around long enough to become the only child youngest, middling's are never alone and thus never get one hundred percent of the parent's investment of time and money." Consequently, the second born usually grows up to be independent in thoughts and actions. That is the character of my sister, Roberta.

Subsequently, based on my acceptance of this analysis, my behavior was contrary to the apparent happy-go-lucky and free spirited traits of my three siblings. Similar to my youngest brother who always looked sad, I was constantly looking for evidence that I could be loved! Although my behavior was not understood by many, including me, their recall described me as an extremely angry child; a child who had a perpetual frown on my face; and finally a child who was perceived as inward and quiet as opposed to outward or verbally expressive. No one knew what I was thinking, but because of my countenance, I was perceived as uncaring, angry, and self-contained. Today, as a result of therapy, formal education, experiences, and self-awareness enhancement opportunities, I now know I felt abandoned, and not yet able to *"move out of my own way."*

Again, as a toddler, walking at the young age of eight months, I was not aware of my mother's prenatal condition of five months and that she was expecting to deliver my sister Olivia in another four months. I also was not aware of the reasons behind my mom's inability to pick me up, coddle me, or hold me in her comforting arms the way she did when I was an infant. I was not aware that my mother's weakened physical health, due to her earlier bout with pneumonia, as well as her protruding belly, were the reasons behind her behavior and my feelings of abandonment.

Apparently, although <u>not</u> breastfed, my first few months of existence must have been reassuring and soothing for me. Otherwise, I would have no means for comparison. Today, I can only imagine the painful feelings of "abandonment" I must have felt when my mother no longer gave me the attention I obviously was accustomed to in feeling safe and secure in the womb. I therefore lost my ability to trust my environment outside of the womb.

I later discovered the concept and repercussions of being considered an "Irish Twin". The term "Irish Twin" is used to describe two children born of the same mother in the same calendar year or within ten to thirteen months of each other. The phrase originated as a derogatory term associated with Irish immigration to the United States and England in the

1800's. The implication at that time was that large groups of close-in-age siblings were the result of uneducated, poor Irish Catholic families' lack of birth control as well as self-control. Although I am actually fourteen months older than my sister, Olivia, I still consider myself an "Irish Twin". The adverse impact my sister's birth had on my emotional and psychological state of well-being did not manifest itself until much later in life. I never considered Olivia as the blame for my behavior. It was simply a relief to understand the root source of my behavior.

Feeling Valued:
My Inherent Need to be Loved

"You did not choose me, but I chose you and appointed you to go and bear fruit – fruit that will last. Then the Father will give you whatever you ask in My name." John 15:16

What people want most in the world is to feel valued, loved, appreciated, cherished, and respected. It is therefore love or lack of love that drives our behavior. How did love shape who I have become? Did feeling or not feeling valued drive my behavior toward who I am today? According to Deborah Anapol, Ph.D. in her book <u>Love without Limits</u>, she states:

"Love is bigger than you are. You can invite love, but you cannot dictate how, when, and where love expresses itself. You can <u>choose</u> to surrender to love, or not, but in the end love strikes like lightening, unpredictable and irrefutable. You can even find yourself loving people you don't like at all. Love does not come with conditions, stipulations, addendums, or codes. Like the sun, love radiates independently of our fears and desires.

...You cannot make someone love you, nor can you prevent it, for any amount of money. Love cannot be imprisoned nor can it be legislated. Love is not a substance, not a commodity, nor even a marketable power source. Love has no territory, no borders, no quantifiable mass or energy output."

Through formal education, individual therapy, and avid research, I am personally able to discern and validate Dr. Anapol's statement that *"Love is bigger than you are."* Some of us were fortunate enough to have received an abundance of healthy love from parents or extended family during our formative years. To the contrary, many of us were psychologically damaged as babies, toddlers or young children because of the lack of love we thrived for as we sought its value. An experience of illness, feelings of abandonment, or even the trauma of the death of a parent or sibling, as well as divorce and remarriage, can have an adverse impact on one's sense of security as we move through the journey of life. Contingent upon the environment, there are others who come into the world not knowing love until they are adults.

Travelling Down Memory Lane

As an adult, I pondered on a childhood experience that helped me to fully appreciate the power of free choice. When I was about eight years old and walked alone down an unfamiliar block in my community, I became stuck and had to make some conscious choices. I was returning home from the "Brownies" which is a guiding organization for young girls aged seven years to ten years old. The block was rather long, unusually quiet, and devoid of traffic as well as people. This was the first time that I can remember when I consciously felt stuck, on my own, and misplaced. My family and I were new to the community as we recently moved from an apartment to a new home. During that time, I did not know the difference between an apartment and a house, as the three-bedroom apartment we lived in was always called "home"! Why I was alone on that particular day, I don't recall. I am the middle child of five and not accustomed to being without at least one sibling. This sense of aloneness on that unforgettable day is why I recall it so poignantly.

The Impact of Negative Pride

Nonetheless, I suddenly realized that I was in unfamiliar territory and did not know what to do about it. Although I was eight years old, I was never educated on the importance of street signs and how to read them. I guess my parents made the assumption that I would learn this on my own or from my siblings. They were partially right; I was now by myself, no siblings around, and had to quickly learn how to navigate the community on my own.

I did see a friendly looking woman walking toward me that I could have approached, but even at the young age of eight, my shyness together with my negative pride got in my way, causing me to walk past her. I stubbornly believed I could do this on my own! As I continued to walk down the street, I suddenly became frightened, anxious, and fearful. I furtively turned around to see how far the friendly looking woman had travelled. Her distance regrettably was too far for me to catch up with her and my negative pride was too big for me to choose to run after her. The more I walked, the more frightened I became. Suddenly, just before the tears were about to roll down my presumed flushed cheeks, I paused at a street light, looked up and realized that there were street signs on each corner with numbers and words on them that at first didn't make sense to me.

The Purpose of Signs

Through this moment of reflection, it appeared to me that the street signs must have a purpose and would give me some sense of where I currently am and where I am to go.

So I followed my instincts and continued to walk to see where the street signs would take me. Well, I walked one block, crossed the street and then walked a second block and a third. Before I knew it, I recognized a street sign that said "108th Street". I looked up and down the street and thankfully saw familiar homes, parked cars, and other comfortable surroundings. I was elated that I was no longer stuck but rather on my way to my destination, home! Dr. Seuss was right when he said:

> *"With your head full of brains*
> *And your shoes on your feet,*
> *You're too smart to go down*
> *Any not so good street."*

Therefore, using my brains, I discovered that signs do have a purpose! I was no longer depressed; I was no longer confused; I was no longer void of direction; I no longer felt lost. I had a purpose and made the choice to move any obstacles that may be in my way! I was now optimistic about what lay ahead. I was going home! I will never forget the relief I felt that afternoon when I used my brains and the gift of free choice to meet my purpose! I ran up my stoop steps, opened the door, and felt the warmth of family that I normally took for granted. What a comfort it was to feel once again secure at home simply because of my ability to use my free choice and to learn how to appreciate the purpose of signs, written as well as spiritual!

Choosing to Become Unstuck

In retrospect, even at age eight, I had a choice to sit on the curb and cry, remain stuck until someone noticed I was lost, or I could choose to keep walking. Today I'm pleased I chose the latter as it was so liberating to move past my fear of being lost. It was so redemptive to *move out of my own way*, even as a child; I felt so free to be in an accustomed environment that is my safety net called home. That day I learned what it felt like to choose to become unstuck. It helped me to recall another quote from Dr. Seuss of which I later taught my children:

> *"You will come to a place where the streets are not marked.*
> *Some windows are lighted. But mostly they're darked.*
> *A place you could sprain both your elbow and chin!*
> *Do you dare to stay out? Do you dare to go in?*
> *How much can you lose? And how much can you win?"*

"Oh, The Places You'll Go!" by Dr. Seuss

Currently, I tend to be adventurous and seek opportunities to explore my surroundings. In other words, I no longer panic when I lose my way. Rather, I pursue the situation with vigor and confidence, recognizing there is always a roadmap, spiritual signs, or posted signs to get me from point A to point B. I just have to believe in myself. As Dr. Martin Luther King once quoted, "Faith is taking the first step even when you don't see the whole staircase."

What did I learn from this experience? I learned four significant lessons about the importance of making wise choices to *move out of my own way*.

First, I learned how important it is to purposefully acknowledge when I feel lost, alone, confused, or humbly stuck. When I am logically aware of my own emotions and learn to speak to it either through self-talk, to God, or to another person, suddenly the unraveling begins, the clouds lift, and the sun is brighter. I now appreciate my focus, persistence, and confidence in achieving a goal when using conscious choice. I've actually *moved out of my own way* and I am generally successful. By not taking my eyes off the prize, it is mine for the asking.

Second, I learned that developing an open mind by *moving out of my own way* is crucial to becoming unstuck. Being open-minded allows me to analyze my circumstances, recognize assumptions, and draw conclusions to make wise choices. Once I became more self-assured in my own abilities as a critical thinker, I easily *moved out of my own way* to use my gift of free choice with confidence.

Third, as a result of my eight-year old childhood experience of being lost, I also learned that there are both "external" and "spiritual" signs in life that I need to pay more attention to whenever I feel stuck, alone, and vulnerable. The external signs are my surroundings that I can see and touch, warning me to take heed, adjust my thinking, and to *move out of my own way*. In other words, I must learn to pay closer attention to things outside of me. The spiritual signs are subtler, since they are based on my intuition, which I call the "Voice of God." These signs can only be heard when I am at peace, still, reflective, humbly sitting or kneeling, or in a meditation mode. It is only when I hear God's direction that I am spiritually able to take action to *move out of my own way*.

Finally, I learned that I must consciously pay attention to my negative pride, arrogance or egocentric thinking. It can become a tripping stone that could prevent me from seeing or experiencing these signs clearly, learning from the lessons, and responding swiftly to the road ahead.

Conscious Choice Leads To Ultimate Control

"Walk with the wise and become wise, for a companion of fools suffers harm." Proverbs 13:20

The word "choice" is described as an action or task of selecting or making a decision when faced with two possibilities. If we don't make a decision, we remain stuck. However, the other option is to make a decision and become unstuck.

Although my eight-year old experience did not lead to a negative outcome, I still had more work to do. My apparent lack of power or freedom of choice to say "no" did not emerge until I was about nine years old. I recall not taking advantage of the choice to say "no" to a relative who was a trusted member of our family. He lived in the rented basement apartment of our home. While my mother and siblings were close by on the first floor, this male relative, who today would be labeled a "pedophile", sexually molested me whenever he got a chance. He would gain permission for me to join him in his apartment where he sexually fondled me more than once. No one but another victim of sexual abuse can relate to the violation of trust I experienced. I trusted my parents to protect me; I also trusted this relative, the child molester, to respect my parents, their home, as well as my innocence.

Because of my upbringing to obey my elders, I never realized that I had the right to say no. As indicated earlier, this inability to recognize my choice to say "no" also happened in the statutory rape encounter with my daughter's father. These traumatic encounters ultimately affected my adult decisions in seeking love later in life. I proceeded with caution.

As a teenager, I did not understand the cadre of options I had in using this gift of free choice. Therefore, I made many mistakes. This level of self-awareness did not truly surface for me until I was in my early thirties. It was around that time in my life that I began associating choice with the control I needed to change my life.

Our Psychological Need for Control

The word "control" is defined as the need to direct the behavior of another person to do what the controlling person wants them to do. In other words, being in control is to have power over a life or someone else's life. Unfortunately, in my first marriage, I was a victim of this type of control over me, so I decided to do something about it. I therefore used my freedom of choice to shape, manage, and control the life I currently have. Learning to ask myself significant questions regarding my past, current status, and what I want my future to look like helped me to better understand that I am responsible for my destiny through the choices I make. I began by consistently evaluating my emotional status with the goal of *moving out of my own way to create a life worth living*.

As part of this self-evaluation, I discovered how others viewed me. I was perceived as a strong-willed, goal-oriented, and controlling person with a mind of my own. I was surprised by these perceptions, but readily accepted them by doing what I could to understand them. My research on being a "controlling person" took me to an abstract of an article that enlightened me to better understand the reasons why I, and others, have this psychological need to control. What I discovered was that my need for control is not a bad thing but rather essential for my well-being. This collaborative article was written by three authors; Laura Leotti, Sheena Iyengar, and Kevin Ochsner. The article is entitled "Born to Choose: The Origins and Value of Our Need to Control." I was fascinated by its content as in one excerpt it stated:

> *"Belief in one's ability to exert control over the environment and to produce desired results is essential for an individual's well-being. It has been repeatedly argued that the perception of control is not only desirable, but it is likely a psychological and biological necessity."*

On Becoming More Self-Aware

After reading this article, I now appreciate my inherent need to use my freedom of choice to control my destiny. It is so satisfying for me to know that I can, without guilt, feel more consciously in control of my behavior and purpose! With this in mind, this abstract has reinforced for me the need for me to believe in myself and *move out of my own way* by deliberately thinking about my possibilities. It has also helped me to recognize and become more aware of the significance behind the power of strength of mind or what is also called "self-control." I've learned that sensible self-control leads to good choices as opposed to the insensible abuse of free choice that normally leads to bad choices.

I used to wonder why I would so often get into debates regarding a steadfast opinion I held close to my heart. Today, I realize that conflict usually surfaced for me when I did not have my own way or exhibit power over a desired result. I also realize that I gravitate to people who have personalities similar to mine, including spouses, friends, coworkers, and managers. Of course, due to my subliminal desire to be with people who have a comparable mindset, we sometimes hit heads due to our psychological need to be in control. In retrospect, my need for control oftentimes generated temper tantrums, bouts of passive-aggressive behavior, belligerent anger, and outspoken comments. However, due to professional counseling, coaching, and experiencing life's challenges, I have learned the importance of not only managing my mouth, but also my emotions. I also realize that if we all want to be in control, I had to learn to let go or relinquish my immediate need to win. I had to learn how to manage my thoughts, my mouth, and my emotions. I have become equipped to follow the necessary steps needed to be more effective in my relationships to *move out of my own way*.

Looking in the Mirror of Truth Through a Fable Called "The Wonderful Wizard of Oz"

"If any of you lack wisdom, he should ask God who gives generously to all without finding fault, and it will be given to him." James 1:5

Remember Dorothy in the children's book and movie, "The Wonderful Wizard of Oz" by L. Frank Baum? As a result of a tornado in her home in Kansas, the author whisked Dorothy's home through space and ultimately transported her and her dog "Toto" to a mysterious place called "Oz". Dorothy, similar to some of my experiences of feeling uncomfortable and stuck, was mystified, confused, frightened and had no directions. Therefore, in order to become unstuck, she had many choices to make.

As Dorothy traveled through foreign territory, she was very frightened and disoriented. As she traveled into the unknown, she discovered there were many strange but friendly looking people called "munchkins". She also ran into a "Wicked Witch of the West" and met the "Good Fairy of the East" in this strange land.

Similarities Between Dorothy and Me

During my journey, I too have met "munchkins" or very friendly people with many differences from me. Some were people with similar values as mine, while others had values that were quite foreign. Nonetheless, this diversity helped me to appreciate the added value differences bring to a relationship.

      I remember my first solo business trip to Bangalore, India. I was unfamiliar with their culture, values, or beliefs. However, I learned very quickly that not only were the people humble, they were also hard workers, accommodating, and a pleasure to be around. Their culture was non-threatening and organized. I discovered we had similar values and beliefs. Throughout my seven-day experience, I was treated with the utmost respect. When my assignment was complete, before going home, I very much wanted to take a sightseeing trip to Mysore, the City of Palaces, which is a famous tourist attraction in India. As a female, my dilemma was whether I should trust such a long trip alone with a tour guide in a country that I've never experienced. Mysore was about a three-hour drive from Bangalore and I had to make a quick choice. Do I allow my fear of the unknown to stand in my way of a new adventure or do I trust the process by *moving out of my own way*. I did not want to later regret this opportunity, so I removed any assumptions by researching and gaining facts about my three-hour excursion. I then evaluated my self-talk of anxiety and placed my safety in God's hands, *moved out of my own way*, and chose to see Mysore, The City of Palaces.

      Upon my arrival in Mysore, I noticed many tourists who were sightseeing like me. There were countless temples and only one church. Before entering each temple, based on culture, I respectfully removed my shoes. Learning about their culture and religion of Hinduism enlightened me. It was explained that Hinduism is actually called the oldest religion in the world and contains a broad range of philosophies bound by shared concepts, linked religions and cultures. Their way of life prescribes to the endless duties of honesty, refraining from injuring living beings, including animals, patience, self-restraint, and compassion. I witnessed the "sacred cows" roaming the streets with their owner, and also the cleanliness of even the smallest living quarters. Their many similarities to me and other Americans were immediately obvious while their differences were few. Like me, they pray often, play with much joy, and place delight in the sumptuous and spicy meals they prepare.

With God by my side, I had a spectacular tour with an attentive driver who not only stayed with me throughout my adventurous tour, he safely returned me back to my hotel without incident. The point here is that there are truly so many good people in the world. Through travels to continents such as Africa, Europe, Latin America, and Asia, I discovered more about myself though my understanding of other people. This education included the People's Republic of China and the country of India, as well as the Caribbean. Like Dorothy, my perspective broadened from these adventurous tourism choices into the unknown.

Undoubtedly, like the "Wicked Witch of the West", both Dorothy and I would be naïve if we didn't accept that many people who may cross our paths may not always have good intentions for us. However, we didn't allow this level of awareness to stunt our ability to take risks so we can grow.

Self-Disclosure is Liberating

If Dorothy wanted to go home, it was recommended by the "Good Fairy of the East" that she follow the "yellow brick road" to talk with the "Wizard of Oz". However, before Dorothy found the "yellow brick road", she met up with her newfound friends: the Scarecrow, the Tin man, and the Lion. To vent her state of confusion and fear, she selectively chose to disclose how she got there; that she was looking for the Wizard of Oz who would help her get back home. She also chose to disclose that she was frightened because she and her dog, Toto, were now lost.

Once trust was established through self-disclosure, the Scarecrow, Tin Man, and the Lion in turn shared with Dorothy their dilemma of being stuck. The Scarecrow says he's uninformed and no one asks or tells him anything; the Tin Man is rusted in place with a serious attitude and just doesn't care about anything anymore; the Lion shared that he had serious anxiety issues and was not only confused most of the time, but also terrified of taking chances. Their problems certainly sounded like some of the problems I encountered when feeling stuck. Which one are you?

Similarities Between The Good Fairy of the East and Me

Similar to the traits of the Good Fairy of the East, I too have had mentors, authentic friends, and people in my life that only had my best interest in mind. Because of one of my learned values to "never air your dirty laundry", I didn't always reveal my life's deepest feelings and confidences. However, once I experienced the emotional release I felt upon self-disclosure to those whom I trusted, it helped me to find my way whenever I felt lost in life.

Becoming Unstuck

Another significant time in my life was when I knew I was stuck and needed help. I was about thirty-two years old at the time. My daughter was a teenager then and we were experiencing many mother-daughter challenges. Due to my dilemma of questioning my skills as a mother, as indicated earlier, I ultimately decided to *move out of my own way* through professional counseling. This was one of the most significant and liberating choices I've ever made. Our subjective self-talk is so constant and often wrong due to lack of discernment and objective responses. In other words, the only voices we generally hear are our own. It has been my experience that we do better when we externalize our thoughts.

Contrary to what many people may think, speaking to an objective professional lifts clouds of confusion. Also, during the seventies, professional counseling was not as popular as it is today. Therefore, my spiritual belief is that God guided me at such a young age to *move out of my own way* by seeking professional help. God was preparing me to create a life worth living.

The Self-Serving Tin Man
"I Don't Care About Anything Anymore"

As a significant part of my emotional development, I had established and nurtured many friendships. A person who I know behaved similar to the "Tin Man". She is a kind and virtuous person, but appeared to be apathetic about the emotional needs of friends. In this person's frame of reference, her friends' needs and desires simply were not on her radar. She did not feel that their concerns were a priority in her life. In other words, she did not place the same weight or value on their needs when they expected attention. The perceptions by others were that her attitude was more self-serving than self-sacrificing.

Perhaps she was right to take a stance regarding her conflicting priorities! She was an extremely busy businesswoman juggling many balls in life. I later learned she had so many family demands in her personal life that her family, as well as her emotional stability were foremost on her mind. Of course, the Tin Man cared about others just as much as my friend cared. As you know, we all have conflicting priorities that may cloud the perceptions of others.

Similarities Between The Self-Serving Tin Man and Me

Similar to the self-serving "Tin Man", I too sometimes had self-serving attitudes that manifested into unfavorable behavior. When I was in my early thirties, working full time and working on my graduate degree after work, my primary focus was on earning my credentials. My daughter was eighteen and my son was thirteen. Today, I recognize that, like the Tin Man, I appeared to be apathetic about the needs of my teenage children. I felt they were old enough and self-sufficient enough to fend for themselves. I was wrong. I simply was not there to help them demystify this vulnerable stage in their young lives. Looking back, they did not consider me a bad mom, but through adult-to-adult discussions, they recognized that I simply had a goal and became blind-sighted as a parent. Like the Tin Man, I did care, but it appeared as though I did not. Consequently, we lost valuable parent-child teaching moments in the most vulnerable time of their lives. They made avoidable mistakes that could have been barred if I had not been so self-serving but rather more attentive to this time in their young lives.

Today, as a result of this experience of introspection, I encourage parents of teenagers who desire to earn a degree part-time after work to postpone their plans. The best time to pursue a degree is either when their children are under the age of puberty, or when they are independent adults.

The Insecure Scarecrow
"Nobody Tells Me Anything"

The next person I think of, when considering the Scarecrow in the story, was an acquaintance of mine who had many feelings and reactions that characterized her as an insecure communicator. She was a caring and sensitive person who would do anything for her family or friends. However, she would lose her temper and become aggressive when she was left out of the loop. Her consistent defensive mode exhibited hurt or a void in her life that was deeply rooted with unresolved issues. On these explosive occasions, she would shift from a soft-spoken, lovable person to an angry and insecure person. She would shut down by becoming withdrawn and passive. Perhaps she was like the "Scarecrow", who sometimes had feelings of alienation whenever he felt unloved, unwanted, or left out.

The Similarities Between the Insecure Scarecrow and Me

Like the "Scarecrow," I too had deeply rooted abandonment issues that made me not only angry as a child, but also aggressive and defensive as an adult. Before I could correct my attitudinal and behavioral problems, I first had to learn how to own them to become more secure and less aggressive.

As with Dorothy, when I acknowledged that I was going through an emotional transition that led me to believe I was stuck, I ultimately took the necessary steps to become unstuck. As the years moved on and I matured, became educated, and trained in the field of psychology, I ultimately discovered through my experiences as a psychologist that my problems were minimal in comparison to other people who also feel stuck, but in denial. It was not until I acknowledged my feelings of abandonment, deficits, and fears, that I was able to *move out of my own way,* feel more secure, and change my behavior. In essence, we can all change our mindsets as no one is in control of them except ourselves.

The Roar of the Lion: "I'm Terrified of Failing"

Similar to the Lion, who was frightened most of the time, I have a girlfriend who was an acute worrier. Like the Lion, she had a big heart and was simply misunderstood because she cared deeply about family and friends. Because of her need to feel responsible for everyone's well-being, she was portrayed as controlling. In her mind's eye, letting people down was not an option and it would cause her to feel like a failure. Comparable to the Lion, I know of a number of people who experience feelings of anxiety and habitual worry, specifically about loved ones. Whenever they were faced with events associated with change or the unknown, they spoke of sleepless nights and anxiety producing worry! They said they felt out of control. Their greatest emotion was the fear of failure.

Similarities Between The Roaring Lion and Me

I was also one of these people who worried, having sleepless nights of the unknown or change. Fortunately, as I matured and understood myself better, I was able to *move out of my own* way by appreciating that: (a) we unnecessarily worry about what we don't know, yet imagine what could happen that exacerbates our worry and, (b) worrying can immobilize us to the point that we do not appreciate that the process of change is linked with progress, advancement, and growth.

As uncomfortable the process of change may be, I've learned that stepping into it is far better than fearing it. When I was in fear or became anxious, I was unable to take any action. When I stepped into my fears, I learned more about *"me"* in preparation for the next occurrence as it is bound to occur again and again. Finding out whatever information I can in regard to my source of worry also reduced my fear and anxiety as worry is generally based on the unknown.

On Becoming Confident, Composed, and Content

Again, like Dorothy, developing an open mind and *moving out of my own way* at different points in my journey of life was crucial for me to become unstuck. Once Dorothy became more confident in her own abilities in helping the Scarecrow, the Tin Man, and the Lion *move out of their own way*, she was no longer depressed, she was no longer confused, she was no longer void of direction, and ultimately, she no longer felt lost. She had a purpose and chose to move any obstacles that may be in her way. She was now optimistic about her future and ultimately travelled to her destination without fear or anxiety. She was looking forward to going home!

Like Dorothy, I too became more confident, composed, and content in my abilities in helping others to *move out of their own way*. By cultivating my true passion of educating, coaching, and counseling those in need, my confidence in who I am slowly escalated. I am no longer the shy, quiet, and reserved young lady I was in my twenties. The Scarecrows, Tin Men, Lions, and Good Fairies of the East whom I met along the way changed that. Although it was an uphill ride to attain my credentials, skills, experiences, and to overcome personal obstacles along the way, I consistently worked on creating a life worth living. Accordingly, I am no longer depressed, confused, or void of direction. I live my life as a confident child of God.

Today I recognize that God guided me to serve Him through my consciously chosen profession of industrial psychology. God has bestowed upon me many gifts that I continue to passionately use and not take for granted. My understanding of the excerpt from the scripture Luke 12:48, "To whom much is given, much is required" demonstrates that I must continue to do His will. I therefore am no longer lost! Again, like Dorothy, I am consistently optimistic about my future and I fervently continue to create a life worth living. I am at peace at home on earth.

Turning the Page

So how did I turn the pages in my life to *move out of my own way* when there is so much unresolved baggage? Introspection was the key that unlocked my "Journey of Life".

As a child, I do remember feeling lost and alone the majority of the time. I generally felt like an outsider in my family, until the birth of my baby brother William. Prior to his birth, my constant companions were my two sisters, but more importantly, my imagination and self-talk.

Unfortunately, as my journey of life continued, many mistakes were made because there was no right or wrong answers to my self-dialogue. My concept of "Freedom of Choice" was so limited that I simply didn't know how to "*move out of my own way*". I thought I had no power to do anything but obey. I was such an angry child who consistently had outbursts of temper tantrums, throwing myself to the floor, filled with rage, kicking, screaming, and uncontrollably sobbing, and today I know the "why" behind my behavior. I unquestionably felt abandoned and lost.

If I had not exercised my spiritual right to free choice and seek the help I desired, my life would have been different. I needed to understand my behavior before I could self-correct and *"move out of my own way"*. I also needed to feel safe and secure if I were to create a life worth living. I realize today I could have ended up void of self-worth, uneducated, in prison, or even dead.

What I truly know today is that **_I am_** a child of God who loves me unconditionally. This spiritual awareness gives me self-confidence, courage, and a passionate yearning to move on to fulfill His wishes as a servant by using all of the talents He graciously bestowed upon me. I wish the same for you.

> "Just don't give up what you are trying to do. Where there is love and inspiration, I don't think you can go wrong."
>
> Ella Fitzgerald

Lesson Five

The Denial Factor: The Painful Process of Looking Within

"Submit yourselves, then to God. Resist the devil, and he will flee from you." James 4:7

So far, you know about my journey, my past, my children, how I sought and found love, and the choices I have made that molded me into whom I am today. This lesson focuses on parts of my existence that caused me to pause and reflect upon segments of my life that have been hidden behind denial factors. This reflection has therefore caused me to go through "The Painful Process of Looking Within".

Over the years, due to my spiritual and Christian development, I believe God is molding me into what He wants me to know, how He wants me to behave, and who He wants me to become. Since I courageously stepped into this journey of self-development, there have been many external signs that were immediately recognized by me as reasons for me to look within. However, I ignored these signs by stepping into the mode of denial as this has not been an easy process for me. In some instances, I acknowledged what I needed to change in my behavior, while in other instances I disregarded this need for behavior modification.

Contingent upon my mindset at the time, I easily became blind to some of the external signs that others could clearly see as an obstacle in my growth and development. We can only accept blame, even self-criticism, when we are ready to hear it, accept it, and grow from it. Today, however, I have learned that for me to be successful in life, I must remain consciously aware of my positive as well as the negative self-talk that extend to my behavior. This painful evolution to becoming a better Christian, servant, wife, mother, professional, citizen, and human being is and will continue to be a work in progress.

 I, like many people, have been conditioned to be subjective rather than objective, secretive in lieu of being transparent, and defensive as opposed to being true to self. In many instances, I have practiced each one of these positions where I now know I have been in denial due to personal bias, predisposition, or inability to accept what I didn't want to know. Perhaps, this lesson on "The Denial Factor: The Painful Process of Looking Within" will also help you to look within and assess your past behavior to determine who you truly are or how you are perceived by others.

 The first entity I needed to work on was my self-talk and the impulsive need to express my thinking without reflection or pause. Not only was my outspoken views and opinions selfishly stated, timing as well as my audience were not consciously taken into consideration. Also, at times the expression of my thoughts was unconsciously stated in an aggressive tone along with antagonistic body language. I discovered that this attitude caused my heartfelt message to sometimes be heard in an aggressive or attacking manner which was not how I intended it to be received. This was prior to my journey of self-discovery. Since then, I've learned that it is not the intent behind my message, but rather the impact that my words have on the listener. Therefore, I must consciously think before I speak.

To Thy Own Self Be True

"The heart is deceitful above all things, and desperately sick; who can understand it? Jeremiah 17:9

How well do we really know ourselves? Are we aware of why we do what we do when we do what we do? When we are upset, are we aware of our feelings or emotions when we say what we say? Are we aware of why we have such an impulsive need to say what we say when we are stating an opinion or comment? If you answered in the affirmative, you are probably one of the few who will be labeled what is called "emotionally intelligent."

Over the last forty years, investigative study and inquiry indicates that only thirty-six percent of people tested in emotional intelligence are able to accurately identify their emotions as they happen. So what does this say about our knowledge of self? We are not very self-aware. Others may see in us what we don't see in ourselves because they are actually looking at us as though we are in a picture frame. As you know, it is difficult for us to clearly see ourselves outside of the picture frame if we are in the picture. Being in the picture deprives us of the objective and unbiased view that others may clearly have us. If we allow them to give us honest and authentic feedback, we become better human beings by having knowledge that gives us the opportunity to self-correct. In principle, many of us lack this understanding of self-awareness and will not give permission to be critiqued or accept another's perception of our behavior.

In 1990, a relatively new concept was introduced to society by two psychologists, John Mayer and Peter Solovey. In

1995 however, it was Daniel Goleman whose international best seller, "Emotional Intelligence" helped the world to understand its importance, especially for educators of "Social and Emotional Learning" programs. Today, in the business world, we also have the opportunity to learn about Emotional Intelligence through training and development programs, the internet, and through reading books.

Emotional Intelligence can be described as the capacity of human beings to recognize their own and other people's emotions, to discriminate between different feelings and brand them appropriately, and to use emotional information to guide thinking and behavior. It has become a guiding curriculum in the workplace today, specifically in leadership training programs, interviewing, and career succession programs. It has also been determined by these researchers and psychologists that the concept of Emotional Intelligence or EQ is rated higher than what we know as IQ, our intelligence quotient. To be successful in today's workplace, if we lack emotional intelligence, it simply doesn't matter how intelligent we think we are. It therefore helps us to respond to and manage our emotions as they surface, including our body language and tone, and to utilize our logical intelligence in a beneficial way.

It has been determined that many of us have limited knowledge of self. This deficit clearly has an adverse impact on our use of conscious choice. I know the conservative statements I want to make to the world through my dress code; I know the type of life partner I want because I know what attracts my attention and who can become my balance; I also know the type of profession I seek; I know the home that meets my needs, and how many children I desire. I also know that I sometimes get nervous just before presenting to a large group. However, if you or I were asked the following thought-provoking questions about our emotional self-knowledge, will we be prepared to answer them in a way that says we know ourselves well?

1. What are three values that drive our behavior today?
2. What are three attributes that we consistently exhibit that friends and family admire?
3. What are three deficits that other people may be aware of that we may deny?

A decade ago, I would not have been able to answer these questions. After learning more about me, my values, strengths, and weaknesses, I became a more confident person. With this level of confidence, I consistently evaluate the need to *move out of my own way* so I can be a more responsible human being. I also discovered that each response to these questions validated my true emotions in my daily interaction with the world.

Learning To Become a Conscious Communicator

As a child, I chose not to speak much. Instead, I had a perpetual frown on my face, revealing my true feelings of confusion, anger, and resentment stemming from my experiences of perceived abandonment as an infant; therefore, the myopic world I lived in experienced my anger and attitudes primarily through my body language. This certainly had an impact on my ability to establish long-lasting relationships. In actuality, as a child, adolescent, and teenager, outside of my sister, Roberta, I only established one childhood friend until I was mature enough to enter into the world of work.

According to documented research initially conducted in 1967 by Albert Mehrabian and Susan Ferris, they discovered that, contrary to popular opinion, our words were not the primary way in which our brain processed communication. In fact, it was determined that our brain is multidimensional and therefore, a high percentage of information verbally conveyed is in a non-verbal manner. Consequently, I learned that when I verbally communicate my opinion or response to a question, contrary to my intent, the brain of the listener first processes my body language, and then hears my tone before it takes in the words. In actuality, the visual component of the message represents about sixty percent of the communication process, the tone of voice captures thirty percent, and our words only represent ten percent. In summary, ninety percent of the communication process revolves around our body language and our tone. Therefore, our choice of words, regardless of our vocabulary, only represents ten percent of what's being heard.

What a powerful learning this lesson in communication has been for me! Contrary to my childhood choice to hardly speak, today I am a public speaker who makes every attempt to be a conscious communicator. When speaking at any given time, I try to be cognizant of my body language, my tone, and of course, the choice of my words.

The Catalyst for Defeat

As much as I introspect on my past, I again reiterate and realize how this emotion called love has had a major impact on my entire life. As previously mentioned, I now realize that the desire for love is not a choice but rather a psychological need that we all have at some point in our lives. Emotionally, it is constantly sought after.

There were times in my life that I used dangerous tactics to fill this basic need for love. Through dysfunctional behavior, both in marriage and while divorced, when I couldn't get my way, I became passive-aggressive. In other words, I had the psychological need to vindictively express myself through silence or non-responsiveness. I discovered I became aggressive primarily through my body language, tone, or through my silence. When I resorted to simply being aggressive by the choice of words I spoke, I did not realize it then, but my body language and tone outweighed my cutting words. I subsequently had to learn to pay attention to my body language first, then my tone, if I truly wanted to be heard.

My Emotional Choices

Through reflection, some of my regrettable emotional choices have already been shared, including compromising my children's safety and happiness in order for me to create a fuller life. While they were teenagers, I worked during the day and chose to attend graduate school in the evenings. Although their physical and security needs were met, I did not give much thought to their emotional needs. While attending classes, I was secure in the fact that they had shelter, food to eat, and at least one parent at home with them; however, through adult conversations with my children, due to their personal challenges, I now realize they needed more parental guidance, moral support, and a sense of stability.

Today, in retrospect, I believe my physical absence caused them more harm than good. When I became a single mom, I realized that this period in their lives was also challenging for them. This was when they were both emotionally lost, feeling insecure, and searching for their respective identities.

In another sense, I also had to evaluate my emotional compulsion to spend money. As both a married woman and single mother, I consistently had more expenses than income. Why? First of all, as part of my value system, I was taught the need for survival included having shelter, food, and clothes, as opposed to management of money through savings and investments for the future. Throughout my adult life, instead of being more responsible with income, I inattentively, yet passionately, managed my finances primarily to provide for and meet my current emotional needs and those of my children. What was the genesis behind these emotional needs and desires?

Internal Reasons

"O Lord my God, I called to you for help and you healed me."
Psalm 30:2

I began my self-discovery journey by reflecting solely on me and my behaviors as a woman of the flesh who, like each of us, is capable of doing wrong, making bad choices, or simply unconsciously living from day to day. I consider this journey of reflection the beginning stages of evaluating the internal reasons for my emotional needs and desires.

This expedition began as a result of me acknowledging the courage it will take to go through this painful process of looking within. I desperately wanted to be authentic, remove any factors of denial, peel back any layers of defense that I am not aware of that could get in my way to being a better servant of God. I therefore chose to review and deeply study my behaviors that are based on the flesh. What I discovered about myself is what most people want… to feel good about me.

This sounds simple, but in actuality most of us don't see ourselves that clearly. We want to be successful in what we do, but we very seldom examine the "whys" behind our behavior. Some of us are unconsciously attempting to meet the expectations of our parents, spouses, children, siblings, or our alter ego, the other you. For me, my journey of self-discovery is an emotional need that is beneath many layers of denial. When sentiments of doubt, guilt, shame, or insecurity surface for any reason, my immediate tendency was at one time to defend them. To move out of my own way, I had to learn to hear and accept feedback without resistance.

External Reasons

"O Lord my God, I called to you for help and you healed me." Psalm 30:2

In most instances, contrary to what I know about myself today, I more readily tended to point to external reasons rather than <u>internal</u> reasons for my poor choices or dysfunctional behavior in life. When there was a poor fit between me and a career opportunity, I felt it was because of the interviewer that I didn't get the promotion. When relationships deteriorated or never began, it had to be some flaw in them. When I experienced financial problems, I simply blamed this deficit on the need for more money as opposed to poor money management. When I was faced with or experienced dysfunctional family issues, it was my parent's fault. In essence, I, at one time, believed there were more external reasons behind these feelings rather than internal reasons. In most instances, I really needed to examine myself by looking within to remove any issues of denial in order to create a future that allowed me to live my life in peace and harmony.

The Power of Introspection

Many of us have negative self-talk. As a result, this self-talk causes us to make wrong choices, causing us to feel less than or inadequate at times. I have since learned to evaluate my emotional status and choices by consistently asking myself significant questions concerning my past, present, and future. I today know that my purpose in life is to use my gift of discernment to coach others to *move out of their own way*. This desire and focus has helped me to recognize that before I can truly help others, I had to get in touch with the "whys" behind my past and present behavior. This is the first step toward *moving out of my own way*. I discovered through this introspection that I had three options or choices that would either enrich my life or destroy it.

Option One

Whenever I have negative self-talk or feel stuck, I can: pause, pray, and prepare myself for what's to come through solitude and introspection. This practice has helped me to create a positive mindset and to develop an optimistic plan of action. This was accomplished by shifting my thinking from negative thoughts of failure in my past to positive thoughts of God-driven successes in my future. By focusing on Option One, I taught myself to re-energize my thinking and enrich my life.

Option Two

Whenever I have negative self-talk or feel stuck, I can: Remain in a state of alienation or discontent by staunchly complaining, grumbling, or protesting about my circumstances, but take no action to change my status quo. By focusing on this option, I will more likely than not distort my vision for success, disillusion friends and family, and destroy any hope of happiness, future opportunities, and ultimately my life.

Option Three

Whenever I have negative self-talk or feel stuck, I can: relinquish, resign, and run from the situation, learn nothing from it, and perhaps repeat the same mistake again and again. By focusing on this option, I will stagnate or limit myself to grow, mature, and to seek opportunities to pursue happiness.

Option One is my only choice! By using option one, pause, pray, and prepare myself for whatever tomorrow brings, I am able to *move out of my own way* to become the person I know I am today. This level of awareness and ability to know that I do have choices precipitated the creation of a life worth living.

What I <u>truly</u> know today is that we all struggle to find a way to manage ourselves within the realm of many of these behaviors, including our *negative pride*. Negative pride is one of our biggest obstacles to self-awareness. We have so many secrets that "Pride" won't allow us to reveal. In itself, through denial, "Pride" can get in the way of consciously accepting the other six shortcomings in our everyday lives: lust, gluttony, envy, greed, anger, and sloth. "Pride", in it's rightly order, is the emotion from which all other emotions arise.

However, I had to learn ways in which to get to know me well enough to "*move out of my own way*". I had to stop being in denial by recognizing that I consistently defended constructive feedback; I had to learn to accept what I do well that are considered my strengths; I had to learn to accept what I can do to improve myself by identifying and receptively owning my weaknesses. I must also be willing to do the inner work necessary to concede my strengths or acknowledge a weakness or limitation in the interest of letting go, salvaging, or maintaining a relationship.

In an attempt to *move out of my own way*, I consciously and diligently work on removing an excessive focus on anything that is self-gratifying. Today, I am conscious of the options or choices I have, and the ability to work hard at evaluating my behavior or avoiding bad behavior altogether. From my experiences, choices are perpetually there for me to process, act upon, and to become whole and complete in God's eyes.

"People often become what they believe themselves to be. If I believe I cannot do something, it makes me incapable of doing it. But when I believe I can, then I acquire the ability to do it even if I didn't have it in the beginning.

Mahatma Gandhi

Lesson Six

"The Spiritual Awakening Journey"

"There is neither Jew nor Greek; there is neither slave nor free; there is no male or female, for you are all one in Jesus Christ." Galatians 3:28

A "spiritual awakening" generally does not occur until there is an impact point in our lives that disrupt our current world. When this realization emerges, our focus in life shifts to gratitude rather than pride for the attributes and achievements we are blessed in receiving. This transition allows us to view the world from a place of understanding and empathy, striving for the well-being of others.

There have been so many impact points in my life that could have literally destroyed me because of the choices I made. However, with God's Divine help and direction, I chose not to commit suicide; I chose not to have a nervous breakdown; I chose not to camouflage my pain through the abuse of alcohol or drugs; and I chose not to run and hide from any shame that I may have felt along my tumultuous journey of life. These were not easy choices, but I chose them because I remember my brother Malvane repeatedly saying, "To thy own self be true." This value statement, together with God's guidance, helped me to focus on my blessings rather than regrets.

During the process of self-development, I ultimately became knowledgeable about ethics, integrity, and morals by allowing myself to become vulnerable. I gained a better understanding of who I am by learning from my mistakes, becoming formally educated and seeking professional help as needed, such as mentorships, clinical therapy, and life coaches. Unfortunately, a portion of my unconscious choices resulted in unalterable penalties and deeply-rooted in long-lasting implications such as becoming:

>A sexually abused child at age nine.
>An unwed mother at age fifteen.
>A high school dropout at age eighteen.
>A confused married woman at age nineteen.
>An abused mother of two at age twenty-five.
>A short-lived, first and final grandmother
>of a physically challenged child at age forty-two.

To the contrary, over a fifty-year journey, the long-lasting benefits or blessings of my conscious choices were:

- Giving birth to my first child at age fifteen and making the mature decision to not give her up for adoption.
- Earning a GED at age twenty-four, the catalyst that helped me to seek and earn a bachelor's degree.
- Choosing to become a cancer survivor rather than death at age thirty-four.
- Relinquishing my nineteen-year marriage and becoming a divorcee at age thirty-eight.
- Earning my Master's degree at age forty.
- Trusting a new relationship and, at age 42, marrying my current husband.
- Earning my Doctor of Education degree at age forty-eight.

- Risking relocation at age fifty-five from my hometown in New York City to Atlanta, Georgia.

Through this spiritual awakening, I have certainly become humble. Humility is cultivated by recognizing that my body is simply the outer shell or vessel in which I represent myself while the soul is a microcosm of who I truly am. Rather than touting my accomplishments from an egotistical perspective, I have learned to present my successes as gifts to the adults I educate; I have also learned to present my successes as gifts to the divine characteristic of my existence. I ultimately have become a servant and role model by not speaking of my accomplishments, but rather just living it.

My First Spiritual Awakening
From GED to Ph.D

"Submit yourselves, then to God. Resist the devil, and he will flee from you." James 4:7

As a person who today has a sincere desire to change my lifestyle, I assessed and then threw out any bad habit that offered temporary gratification; i.e., spending unnecessary money, excessive entertaining, eating favorite foods, and watching television. Instead, as a result of this assessment, I prefer to settle for a lasting satisfaction of the spirit. This fulfillment can be found through self-knowledge, self-control, and focus. I used these three gifts of insight to create a new life, one that can be lived with honor and humility. I unknowingly began this journey as a young woman, but lacked the self-awareness to acknowledge my level of self-control and discernment.

In 1967, at age twenty-four, I was tested as a woman, wife, and mother in the business world by my boss, but didn't realize I was being spiritually evaluated until much later in life. I was employed in mid-town Manhattan in a lackluster position as an administrative assistant at a collection agency earning about sixty dollars a week. After about four years of employment, my young boss who was probably a few years older than me began pursuing me sexually. Prior to this initial carnal advancement, we always had a courteous, respectful, and professional relationship; I was therefore very surprised by his promiscuous actions.

He was married and a father; I was married and a mother. One day while everyone was out to lunch except him and me, he grabbed me in the file room, pulled me close to him, wrapped his arms around me, and made his first attempt to kiss me. This initial attempt was the first of many attempts, requiring self-control on my part, causing him to pursue even harder, all of which were in vain. When his attempts to pursue me became even more frequent, I continued to resist. This was very disturbing for me as I was not sure how to manage myself. Somehow, through my resistance and level of self-control, he chose another tactic. Whenever we were alone, he continued to follow me and harass me by making generous compliments, words of endearment, and requests to take me out to dinner and a show. He wouldn't let up. He was truly trying to get to know me personally and romantically. Ultimately his behavior became more persistent and officially transformed into what today is known as "sexual harassment". Being young and a two-prong minority, a woman, and an African American, I chose to not take a position. I knew if I complained, the odds will be against me; I chose not to share this dilemma with my husband, but instinctively knew it was time for me to move on.

I speak to this traumatic time in my life because I believe I was being prepared for the next door I entered. For months, my level of self-control and ability to recognize that I had choices changed my entire life for the better. I could stay and condone this behavior by doing nothing; I could report him to his father who was the proprietor; or I could sever the relationship by quitting my job and seeking other opportunities of employment. I chose the latter. Through reflection many years later, I realize this was another spiritual awakening. God was testing my character.

The Real World of Work

I subsequently applied for a new position. I was immediately accepted as an administrative assistant at a blue chip organization located in midtown Manhattan. It was here that I had a paradigm shift about the world of work and what it required to be successful: it is called "self-achievement". After about two weeks of working in this prestigious organization, God was again at work in my life. A representative from the Department of Career Development approached me in my office space. As part of her job, we conversed about my career aspirations, talents, and dreams for self-development. She also pointed out that the company encourages education and sponsors a tuition reimbursement program. At the end of the conversation, the representative pointed to a line where I was to sign my name. While doing so, I happened to notice the retirement date was not until July in the twenty-first century. We were in the month of August and the year was 1969. This must be a mistake! I couldn't believe what I was seeing. How I translated or deciphered this information in that moment was an awareness of what the "Real World of Work" was about. I was expected to work doing what I was doing into the next century and beyond! At the young age of twenty-two, this was unimaginable and a hard pill to swallow. If my life was going to be filled each day with going to a "job", I knew I had to find my passion.

  This was the first step into my "Spiritual Awakening" Journey. It was this jolt or awakening that led me to be more self-aware and discerning. Today, I now realize I used self-control to thwart off provocations by my boss that could have resulted into a deceitful behavior toward my husband as well as losing my self-respect. Over the years, I kept asking myself what would have happened if I had been naïve enough to be influenced by my boss's charm and met his expectation of having a romantic interlude.

  It was also the conversation with the Career Development agent and the signed document that precipitated my decision to take hold of my "life-reins", change my current direction, and steer in the path of fulfilling a passion verses holding a "job". I intuitively knew in order to become a professional "anything" I needed to earn a college degree. I similarly knew that a criterion to attending college was a high school diploma, which I did not have at this time. Immediately, the wheels started turning and in three months, I earned my

GED. This not only led to my bachelor's degree in psychology, but two advanced degrees.

My current profession allows me to demonstrate my gratitude of my ability to create a life worth living through these "spiritual awakenings. Through discernment and surviving death, I today share my wisdom to leaders, managers, and professionals who sit before me nationally as well as internationally. I am truly humbled by these opportunities.

My Second Spiritual Awakening: A Cancer Survivor at Age 34

"Heal me, O Lord, and I shall be healed; Save me, and I shall be saved, for you are my praise." Jeremiah 17:14

Through a life threatening illness, I encountered my second spiritual awakening, profoundly introducing me to the significance of humility. When I was thirty-four years old and married for sixteen years, I was diagnosed with cervical cancer. According to a research conducted by Dr. Silva Franceschi, "Having sex at an early age can double the risk of developing cervical cancer, a study of 20,000 women suggests." As mentioned, I was fourteen and a virgin when I had my first sexual experience through statutory rape by a man of twenty-two years of age. This unconscious choice, if it can be considered a choice, resulted in the pregnancy of a frightened little girl who knew nothing about sex, life, or the world. The study also noted, "The age at which a woman had her first baby was also an important factor." The point here is that cancer invaded my body, perhaps due to statutory rape resulting in early sexual relations, and childbirth at a young age. Since I was not promiscuous, what was God saying to me? What was He preparing me to do with my young life?

    Being diagnosed with cancer at such a young age rocked my world. I was only thirty-four years old when I received this diagnosis that I had stage four cervical cancer. Because it was so advanced, my life was at stake. To my surprise, I also discovered I was pregnant with my third child at the time and was given the devastating option to have an abortion or risk death. At that time, legal abortion was relatively new in America. I was therefore not psychologically or emotionally prepared for this shocking news. Without thought, my immediate response was to save my unborn child. My primary thought was how would I be able to live with myself if I choose to terminate my child's life before it even begins? I do have a choice. What if the doctor is wrong? I knew this was a risk, but I was willing to take it by not granting permission to abort my child. My daughter, Myishia, was fourteen years old, and my son, J.R., was only nine. They were maturing and so was I. At thirty-four, I knew my biological clock was ticking, so I was ready for a third child in my life.

    Gary, my husband at the time, talked me out of my initial decision. He helped me to understand that I had to make an alternate decision. He reminded me of the other three loved ones in my life: he and my two living children. He asked two significant questions: "What will happen to each of us if you choose to take the risk of carrying my child and neither of you survive?", and "What type of life will we have in your absence as a wife and mother?" After due diligence and God's guidance, I made the choice of having the abortion for the sake of my current family. Under the medical advice of my physician, my decision was affirmed by all involved. While I was on the operating table, just before going under, I felt God's spirit. I knew God was with me all the way during this significant crossroad in my life.

Another Crossroad

This was a time in my life I will never forget. Although I remorsefully ended my child's life, I had another crossroad to bear; I was still experiencing gynecological problems. Fortunately, a close friend of mine became concerned with my on-going physical condition and suggested I get a second opinion. Upon her recommendation, I met with her gynecologist and explained my health issues, my recent abortion, and personal history. His reaction to what I shared was so strong that I became frightened. After receiving the name of my previous "Fifth Avenue" gynecologist, for the purpose of retrieving my records, he admitted me into the hospital that very day. He immediately made arrangements for a cone biopsy the next morning, and subsequently shared with me the results of the biopsy and his diagnosis.

The cancer was at stage four and I must immediately have surgery. After a hysterectomy was performed, I remained in the hospital for one week, recuperated, and reflected on my life for six weeks at home. Again I realized how close to death I was. This was truly another spiritual awakening for me.

Pausing to Reflect

While recuperating, I reflected on my life and how it began to take form as a young woman. At fourteen, as the reality of my pregnancy set in, I knew I was stuck and ultimately decided to become unstuck by applying conscious choice. I chose to keep my secret to myself, often thought of suicide, and lived in fear for nine whole months. My only concern: What will my parents think of me? What will God think of me? Once my daughter was born, however, God was right there beside me, leading me, guiding me, and filling me with His spirit. He helped me to make the necessary choices that would not interfere with the use of my spiritual right to control my destiny. I believe He was creating me to become one of His "special" servants on earth. In order to touch my destiny, God knew my heart and soul. He knew if I were to keep my sanity, my focus, and my tenacious spirit, I had to know He was with me.

Although I was only fifteen, God knew and guided me to make the right decision. He knew I would search the world if my daughter had been taken from me. He created me; He truly knows my heart; He therefore immediately executed His plans for my future, which included Myishia's future. Everything that happened in my life since that first spiritual awakening was the beginning of His mold of my life and my daughter's life.

This period of reflection brought me closer to the realization that God had plans for me, as a mortal human being to do more of His work. I was humbled, grateful, and today I literally see life very differently than I did before this major manifestation.

My Third Spiritual Awakening
Earning My Master's Degree

"How much better to get wisdom than gold! To get understanding is to be chosen rather than silver." Proverbs 16:16

After graduating with my bachelor's degree, I realized how self-assured I had become in who I am as a woman. I became more self-aware which led to the confidence I needed to create a life worth living. To continue on this "spiritual awakening" journey, still employed by this blue-chip organization, I decided to take advantage of their tuition reimbursement employee benefit program and pursue a Master's Degree in Organization Development. Again, God was leading me, guiding me, and filling me with His Holy Spirit.

I had applied at several graduate degree programs, but my first choice would have been Teacher's College at Columbia University. Although I was accepted at several colleges, I didn't hear from Columbia until the Saturday morning, two days before registration began on the following Monday. Upon opening, reading, and processing this memorable acceptance letter, I knew in that moment that God had divine plans for me beyond my understanding. I proudly graduated from Columbia University, School of Education, in May, 1983.

Many years later, I discovered that I was privileged to be on the same dais with President Barack Hussein Obama who graduated with his Bachelor's Degree on the identical day that I did. He was yet to be president of the United States, but today I am humbled simply knowing and honoring this divine occurrence. I learned about this new knowledge directly from President Obama's office when I received a friend request from him while I was at a club in downtown Atlanta. I literally screamed when I read his Facebook "Friend Request" stating that we had both graduated from Columbia University in May 1983. I was truly humbled by this notification.

My Fourth Spiritual Awakening: Earning My Doctoral Degree

"Keep hold of instruction; do not let go; guard her, for she is your life.
Proverbs 4:13

My first thought of the possibility of earning my doctorate was when I graduated from Columbia. It was at this time I witnessed firsthand doctoral graduating students donning their hoods and distinguished regalia. It was a very inspirational experience. After that event and celebration, although inspiring, I was so relieved to move on, apply what I have learned and know, I lost my desire to pursue a higher degree. At that time in my life, I had no vision of earning a doctoral degree. I simply wanted to enter into the professional world of work.

Nonetheless, I guess due to my conditioning as a life-long learner, I still registered and attended post-graduate courses at Columbia University at a whopping non-reimbursable four hundred dollars a credit. That was in the eighties. I wonder what the cost of higher education per credit is today. During this time, I was questioned by a co-student as to why I'm taking post graduate courses without being matriculated toward my doctoral degree. Being matriculated simply means being registered for a specific degree. Her question made sense to me and at that moment a seed was planted.

That awakening was the springboard toward earning a post-graduate degree. The only setback I experienced at the time was that Columbia University did not have a Doctoral Degree Program in Organization Development. Nonetheless, I prepared myself through a process of calmness and concentration and decided that I could focus on a similar curriculum at Columbia.

Again, God intervened. The Saturday that I was scheduled to take the Graduate Record Exam (GRE), as a prerequisite to being accepted at Columbia was the same day that I was to attend a company-related leadership seminar. The forum was a three-day process, including Saturday. I therefore notified the seminar leader in advance about the conflict I had on Saturday morning. She became very interested in my pursuit in earning my doctorate.

Through this divine intervention, I discovered she was the Dean at the University of Massachusetts at Amherst (UMass), School of Education. Subsequently, during that conversation, she invited me to apply for entrance into their Doctoral Program in Industrial Psychology. I was taken aback by this request as I lived in New York which was approximately four hours driving time or close to two hundred miles away from New York City. I therefore declined her offer. I could not fathom or envision the reality of this offer ever coming into fruition unless I relocated. Nevertheless, a few months later and a week before the registration process began at UMass, I received a call from the Dean. I remember this Friday morning very well. She closed the conversation by stating she will do everything possible to delay the selection and enrollment process until all of my documents are received. By the time the conversation ended, in order to meet the University's requirements, I immediately went into action. I excitedly took off from work the rest of the afternoon. The Dean influenced me to submit my application, request and send my transcripts from both my undergraduate and graduate schools that very afternoon. By the end of the day, exhausted but successful, I physically received from each college in question my transcript.

Subsequently, all documents, including my transcripts, were in her office in a couple of days. A few weeks later I received the acceptance letter. Over a two-year period, somehow I managed to drive or take a bus to classes as needed. The year was 1985. I earned my doctorate in 1991.

My First Guardian Angel: My Surgeon

"Behold, I send an angel before you to guard you on the way to and to bring you to the place that I have prepared." Exodus 23:20

God has a way of giving His children the time required to build character in those who lose focus on their goals and aspirations. I was one of His children who experienced setbacks, obstacles, and impediments between 1985 and 1991. My first year at the University of Massachusetts was exciting, inspiring, and also tiring. Not only was I career oriented, receiving advancement promotions at work in title and compensation, and more responsibilities, I was also in a committed relationship with plans to remarry. It was around 1986 that I was hurt on the job which resulted in a major setback. I was diagnosed with a herniated disc which was not only painful, but debilitating. After a series of visits to chiropractors, it was determined that I needed to stay in a prone position for six weeks in order for me to heal. My fiancé proved his love and loyalty during this traumatic time in our lives as he had to do everything for me as though I was an invalid. In actuality, I was an invalid as I was in an "L" shaped position and consistently in pain even when in a prone position. As mentioned in a previous lesson, my fiancé at that time was my nurse, anchor, crutch, and cook during these tumultuous times. Through it all, he hung in there to the end.

After the long and arduous six weeks of conservative therapy, I was still in the same condition, if not worse. It was then determined by the specialists that if I did not have the recommended surgery, I could end up paralyzed for life. Again, another significant choice had to be made. Fortunately, God was with me when I had my initial discussion with the passionate and dedicated surgeon who would perform the procedure. God guided him. He was affiliated with the Hospital for Special Surgery in New York City and shared with me that he does not accept Workman Compensation cases, but to my delight, he chose to do it for me. I would be his first case.

He also introduced me to the concept of a new microsurgery procedure offered to back surgery patients. He said that my incision will be only two inches long as opposed to opening the back completely, leaving a six to nine-inch scar, and perhaps future incidents of pain and distress. This was my primary fear and why I initially didn't want surgery. He also helped me to understand that my prognosis will be more favorable because of this progressive type of procedure. He was right. Thirty-one years later, I am still standing tall and moving through my life without pain. What a blessing. Not only did he create a "brand new me", standing tall a few weeks after surgery, but I was also able to resume work, continue graduate studies, and prepare for my wedding. How did I find this qualified surgeon? He was truly my "Guardian Angel".

Selfless-Unconditional Love
My Second Guardian Angel: Peggy

"For He will command his angels concerning you to guard you in all your ways." Psalm 91:11

The demands of being a newlywed, managing a new home and my career, were simply overwhelming. I was literally putting in seventy hours per week, compromising my focus, my health, and my husband. Something had to give, so my choice was to place my graduate studies on hold. Although I had completed most of the core courses that were required, I still had a few more to complete as well as choose my doctorial committee, and finally write my dissertation. Just thinking about these commitments was overpowering. As many of us may do, we have a tendency to prioritize our work demands before meeting our personal goals.

Fortunately, through the networks I had established at work since 1983, I was noticed by a number of executives who observed my competence, work ethics, level of integrity, and interpersonal skills. While at this organization, I was promoted five different times, each more demanding than the last. However, there was one person, my second guardian angel, who was an ex-nun who joined the organization as a Vice President. At the approximate age of fifty-three, since leaving the convent, this was her first position in the corporate world. I interacted with her on a number of occasions during meetings and training sessions and instantly liked her. She was a soft-spoken, intelligent, humorous, yet caring person. Ultimately, she and I developed more than a professional relationship. We actually became friends as I am still in touch with her today.

  One day, I received an interesting call from her. She offered me an opportunity to work in a key position directly with her. After discussing the organizational development duties of which I became excited, she then gave me a contingency. This is when I knew she was my guardian angel. She said she would like to offer me the position with a generous salary increase, but I must promise her I will complete my doctorate. What an offer! What a contingency! I was truly elated and so grateful. I accepted the position and she thoroughly supported me by allowing me to attend classes at UMass as needed. We agreed that I would use my vacation days whenever I attended classes during the work week.

  One example of my schedule, I would leave work on Monday night, go home, and then my husband would drive me to the Port Authority Bus Terminal in Manhattan. There, I would catch a midnight bus, attend 9:00 AM classes on both Tuesday and Wednesday and return home that evening on the 4 PM bus. I would then promptly return to work on Thursday morning. This is only one example of the latitude Peggy afforded me and the discipline and self-control I applied during this challenging time in my life. She also gave me the autonomy to stay at work as late as I needed to write my dissertation. Without her selflessness and unconditional love, I may not have earned my second advanced degree in 1991. Where did she come from? For the second time, I recognized that I have been blessed with the divine intervention of another guardian angel.

My Third Guardian Angel: Linnette
"And whatever you ask in prayer, you will receive, if you have faith."
Matthew 21:22

During my professional career, I was hired as Director of Training and Development in a conglomerate organization employing over fifty thousand people. After earning my doctorate, in addition to my typical duties, I was often a consultant for some of the executives. One woman executive, whom I was contracted as a consultant, befriended me and opened many doors for me. As the years passed by, she was advanced to even higher positions. Subsequently, she broadened my exposure and gave me opportunities as a consultant to one of the greatest professional training grounds in the City of New York…a trauma hospital and its facilities. Because of her, I facilitated training sessions for the Community Board, Executive Staff, physicians, clinicians, and professional as well as union staff. I also was exposed to challenging decision opportunities such as downsizing, budget freezes, reorganizations, and cultural changes. I learned so much from this experience while employed there for fourteen years. My last position in this organization was under her leadership as

Executive Deputy Director. She was also my mentor, confidante, and friend. We are still in relationship today.

Currently, nationally and internationally, I use many anecdotes from these experiences in my current training sessions that I facilitate. From this guardian angel, I learned what to do as a leader, and of course, what not to do. God placed Linnette in my life for a reason.

In closing this lesson, I have been enlightened through my spiritual awakening journey as well as by sending me three guardian angels. Since spiritual signs are not accessible to me on an everyday basis, I've noticed that when I hear God's voice, it generally happens when I am in the throes of distress or a setback. It is perceived as a spiritual sign because no one can hear my thoughts or this mental dialogue but God. It is at this juncture I seek God's divine or transcendent intervention. Once I began to recognize the importance of paying attention to spiritual signs that resonated from within, I heard the voices in my head that were positive, recurring, constructive, risky, and action-oriented. I discovered that the voices are spiritual when they tell me to do something that I normally will not do without this Divine intervention.

Since I am today aware that these spiritual awakenings happened for me, I know I have created a life worth living.

"When I am secure in Christ, I can afford a risk in my life. Only the insecure cannot afford to risk failure. The secure…can admit failure…seek help and try again."

John Maxwell

Lesson Seven

Keeping God First: Maintaining a Life Worth Living

"Submit yourselves, then to God. Resist the devil, and he will flee from you." James 4:7

Much thought has been given to the number of lessons I desired to share with you in this spiritual autobiography. I vacillated among the numbers "five", "six" or "seven" lessons, but had my heart set on "seven" because of its meaning. The number seven in the bible represents completeness, divine perfection, totality, and is mentioned at least four hundred and ninety times through scripture. Therefore, this Seventh lesson on "Keeping God First: Maintaining a Life Worth Living" is the result of my mental debate. I'm at the place in life where Keeping God First is simply a given.

Through all of life's curves, dangerous roadways, and dark tunnels, I've learned to "Keep God First" as my constant focus in everyday life. When I wake in the morning, I keep Him first; when I get into my car, I keep Him first; when I prepare myself to begin another day, I keep Him first. Before each training session, I keep Him first by getting on my knees, humbly asking Him to send the right people into my training sessions and to give me the right messages that they need to hear. When I close my eyes at night, I keep Him first.

In this lesson, I will speak to God's goodness in answering my prayers when He felt I was ready to hear it. I will

also share with you how God has answered my specific prayer in my quest to "Maintain a
Life Worth Living" by the relocation of twenty-seven members of my family. Throughout my life, even with its ups and downs, family has been the nucleus of my mortal being.

In this final lesson, I will first share with you how my unwavering faith in God carried my husband and me through a serious setback in our lives. I will then close this lesson with my family's' Relocation Chronology. My purpose is to help you move out of your own way by appreciating God's Divine intervention when we need Him, and of course, appreciating the unconditional love of family that many of us take for granted. Even with our distinct personalities, sibling rivalry, and sometimes feelings of betrayal, it is always good to know they are close by when we need them.

My Unwavering Faith in God

God answers prayers in his own time. Today, I have an unwavering faith in Him because whenever I seek His help, He is there making things happen. He has always answered my prayers, but only in His due time. He knew when I was ready to receive His help. It took years for me to process, accept, and live my life with this spiritual level of understanding, but today my faith is unwavering.

A few years ago, I know God spoke to me during a traumatic experience worthy of sharing with you. During this unpleasant time in my life, "Keeping God First" blessed both Roland and I as a married couple. In the midst of the economic downturn between 2008 and 2012, Roland and I experienced major life challenges where our faith had been tested more than once. However, as a result of this horrific four-year experience, our character and morals have been further developed as we both unequivocally learned that God is always in control.

Prior to 2008, Roland and I travelled often, shopped as though we had a fountain of funds, and used credit cards like it was going out of style. In essence, we became slaves to our debtors. Consequently, during the next four years, we suffered through the reality of having too much debt and not enough income. Although enjoyable, the bad habits created and established by both of us over the previous years resulted in this realism.

Roland is and always has been a praying man; however, relying on his sixth sense, his intuition, he can become anxious and worrisome at times. I on the other hand, in the present most of the time rely on my five senses more than my sixth sense. I therefore consistently demonstrate my faith in God's infinite wisdom by living in the "Now". Over the years, I trained myself not to worry by placing my concerns in God's hands. Logically, I understand that worrying focuses more on our thinking and our imagination of what *could* happen rather than what *will* happen. In actuality, we don't know what will happen until it actually happens. Only God know this. Therefore, I tend to be more spiritually based and rely on God's guidance. Knowing that I cannot take emotions into my training forums, I have learned to keep God first by staying in the present, causing me not to worry in most forums.

The major setback that caused serious introspection on our behavior was when our bank accused us of being behind in our mortgage payments. Although it was a financial as well as emotional strain for Roland and I to meet all of our liabilities on time, we emphatically knew this was not correct as we have never been late with our mortgage. I almost discounted the entire notion that our house was in jeopardy until Roland became seriously concerned. He couldn't sleep most nights and was in a worried and bothered state more often than not. Due to his sleepless nights, he ultimately helped me to become more grounded in this reality by exposing me to the number of televised people who lost their homes on the courthouse steps in Atlanta, Georgia. To my surprise and disbelief, many of them were also victims of false accusations by major banks which were their mortgage holders. Roland's intuition was on point. This was definitely a warning sign that we had to stay on top of our vulnerable position. The power was not in our hands!

When our bank notified us that our house was in jeopardy due to lateness on our mortgage payments, Roland and I kept God first throughout this entire ordeal. Roland, being in both the banking and mortgage industries at one time in his career, maintained copious banking records and knew he would be able to counter their claim of mortgage payment lateness. After retaining a lawyer, the eight-month process began. Each morning we began our day with prayer, even though our emotions were different. While Roland did the worrying, I kept God first. Each time we went to court. I remained composed and confident that the outcome would be favorable. As previously stated, I knew our home was protected, not only because of our proof, but when I began paying attention to the constant spiritual signs.

I travel often, nationally and internationally, and know well in advance my quarterly schedule. By not showing up on the assigned court date could have been a major setback for us. First and foremost, none of the scheduled court dates conflicted with any of my consultant assignments. This had to be more than coincidence or luck; God simply had our backs. During our travels to and from the courthouse, God also provided us with His Divine traveling mercies. God was with us each time we traveled to the courthouse, as we were never late for our set date and time on the courthouse's docket.

After consultations with our lawyer, attending numerous court hearings, and witnessing the bank's inability to prove their accusation, eight months later the dispute was settled in our favor. When it was all said and done, our bank had to turn over a check to us in excess of $10,000 and reconcile their records to show our creditworthiness. God also provided us with the right judge, a legal support team, including a court-appointed representative from the Justice Department, which led us to this positive outcome.

As I now understand from our lawyer, the bank was aware that our house was more than fifty percent paid off. During this time of industry greed and uncertainty, many banks simply wanted to foreclose on homes to sell for profit and would do anything to attain this goal, even at the expense of innocent people. Roland and I were one of the victims of this scam. However, keeping God first saved us from being homeless during this unsettling time in our lives.

Once we moved past this devastating period, we learned valuable lessons from this experience and vowed never to subject ourselves to an ordeal like that again. We subsequently modified our spending habits, our mindset, and our behavior by reducing our time in restaurants, recognizing that instant gratification of material needs is unnecessary, and began to manage our finances more effectively. More importantly, we immediately put a plan in motion to accelerate our mortgage payments with the sole purpose of owning our home. We now use only cash or debit cards for all purchases and will never be slaves to debt again. Thank you, Father! Today, in keeping God first, we are able to read the spiritual sign that says, "Cash is King."

So far, God has heard my prayers and answered me in each setback in my life. He has also kept me balanced in all I do, including giving me the gift of discernment. He has enlightened me through my spiritual awakening journey as well as sending me three guardian angels. Since I am today aware of these spiritual awakenings, I know I have created a life worth living.

Maintaining A Life Worth Living

As you have read so far, my family is very important to me. Many years ago, my sister Roberta and I deliberated on the significance of being surrounded by family in our retirement or golden years. Neither one of us imposed our dreams on other family members, but again God answered our prayers. We, without collusion, but rather pleaded separately, asked God to orchestrate His divine powers in the relocation of our siblings and their families to Atlanta, Georgia where Roland and I currently reside.

I believe I have already *created* a life worth living primarily because I am consistently at peace. Because of God's continuous response to my prayers, my life has meaningfully been actualized, completed, and *maintained* through the unconditional love and the nearness of my family. We are now all in the State of Georgia.

My Family's Relocation Chronology in Creating "The Circle of Love"

"Trust in the Lord with all your heart. Never rely on what you think you know. Remember the Lord in everything you do and he will show you the right way." Proverbs 3: 5-6

As we age, most of us have a preference to be with family. Therefore, I will share with you how Roland and I ended up in Georgia and how twenty-five members of my family also made decisions to leave New York, relocate to other states, yet now live within an average of twenty-minutes of each other's residences.

Christmas in New York

Remembering Christmas in New York fills my heart with mesmerizing memoirs. Not only was the month of December a beautiful time of the year nationally, New York's crisp white snow-layered tree branches, rooftops, and landscapes caused the atmosphere to have a spiritual feel to it, adding to its wonder. Homes were brightly decorated with Christmas ornaments, neighbors appeared to be warmer and friendlier, chimney smoke ascended toward the sky, and a display of excitement leading up to Jesus Christ's Birthday serendipitously filled the air.

Inside our home, we would play holiday music, trim the Christmas tree together, and then wait on Christmas Eve for my father and sometimes "Uncle Joe" to show up with shopping bags filled with gifts. Most of them were elegantly wrapped in shiny colors; vivid reds, bright greens, and deep purples. Additionally, the mysterious packages were enhanced with large, beautifully tied ribbons and bows to match the color of the gift-wrapped boxes. Because "Uncle Joe" was in the window dressing business for Gimbel's, a major New York department store at the time, our Christmas tree was loaded with stunning packaged gifts. I personally found Christmas Eve more exciting than Christmas morning. The anticipation of discovering what those magical gift boxes held was so exhilarating!

Through the years, as adults and married with children, Christmas remained "Broadway" spectacular at our house. For weeks prior to the occasion, we all looked forward to dining at my mother's house. Maya had an unusually huge kitchen…the same kitchen that we dined in together as children. During these festive holidays, the doorbell didn't stop ringing. In addition to our family members, Malvane had quite a following of childhood male friends who also joined us. If they were married, they generally came alone and were included in our family celebration. Through the kitchen threshold they came, one after another, carrying their "brown bag" under their arm.

This portal to the gathering room, the kitchen continuously welcomed another person to join us, either for dinner or simply to socialize. As the evening progressed, the spirits were plentiful, causing the atmosphere to be filled with feisty and free-willed conversations, hip-moving dancing, and tons of laughter and innocent fun.

As my father and Uncle Joe aged, they seemed to have a desire to be around our large family at every opportunity. Needless to say, with their presence, the family alone was large enough to have one great big party amongst us. Malvane and his wife had two girls, Marie and Lillian; Roberta and her husband had three children: their oldest son, Billy, and a set of fraternal twins, Elizabeth and Levertis, Jr. Gary and I attended with our two children, Myishia and J.R.. My youngest brother, William, who was unmarried, was always in attendance. Unfortunately, my sister, Olivia and her family were living in California during these momentous occasions, so they missed these historic holiday family gatherings.

To say the least, the holidays at my mother's house, including Thanksgiving, Christmas, New Year's Eve, Easter Sunday, Mother's Day, Memorial Day, the Fourth of July, and Labor Day were filled with an abundance of people, food, spirits, laughter, music, and dancing. What warm and enchanting memories. Holiday celebrations were definitely part of our family culture and still are. It was this spirit of family unity that initiated our "Circle of Love" legacy.

The Deal Breaker

During our younger years, our siblings, children, nieces and nephews lived, played, and became educated in the suburbs of New York City. We were relatively close in proximity to each other, but were busy with work and raising families. Therefore, we didn't see each other as often as we would have liked. As expressed earlier, holidays were the events of the year where we would congregate, laugh, dance, have photo shoots, eat, drink, and then depart from each other until the next festive occasion: Christmas, Easter, Birthdays, or Thanksgiving.

Despite the family connections and celebrations, I began to realize that New York City was a constant struggle for me. I had nothing in which to compare my experiences with of traveling daily on hot crowded subways, managing the high cost of living, and constantly thinking about potential crime factors. The city, as well as certain areas of the suburbs, is rampant with twenty-five story high-rise buildings and scattered with public transportation like subways, buses, and taxies. Subsequently, these and other adverse characteristics such as the city's unusually short, hot, and humid summers and its long, arduous, and frigid winters caused my sister Roberta and I to dream about leaving New York.

Roberta and I are two years apart and have always been close as siblings. As we matured, given our quest for warm and sunny skies, she and I travelled together often on vacations to sunny areas that promoted beaches, palm trees, and sunny blue skies. We loved going to the Caribbean Islands, Florida, and Mexico. These trips were the beginning of a "New York City Deal Breaker" for both of us. It was during these trips that we started planning for a less demanding life. It was time to relocate to a less stressful and warmer environment.

She and I spent a good deal of our time together talking about our future and our vision to have our families retire in a place where we could all be in close proximity of one another. We wanted to create a "Circle of Love" in a place where we would spend time together in a warmer and less stressful environment. Since we never experienced the region of the world that had often been characterized as the "Deep South" in family lore and history, we had no idea that our dreams of relocating could actually exist in what has emerged as the "New South".

Leaving New York City

New York City is an adventurous, exciting and wealthy metropolitan region filled with activity twenty-four hours a day. It is bursting with approximately 8.5 million people and is considered to be the most populous city in the United States. During my prime days as a young adult, I loved what I knew about New York and what it had to offer. I must say, having no other perspective, I enjoyed New York's diverse culture, anticipated four seasons, exciting night life, and the hustle and bustle of its crowded streets, specifically in midtown Manhattan.

As I progressed in life, from my new and more mature lens of evaluating tomorrow, my emphasis shifted from adventure and immediate satisfaction to a perspective on the importance of quality of life. For some unknown reason, I began to develop an unexplainable fear that I would die in New

York. I knew in my heart it was time to leave my place of birth.

Today, I know that God was tugging at my heart. Not only did our dream to become a family unit in one location become actualized, we created "The Circle of Love" legacy. As you read on, you will learn about the sequence of chronological events that led up to my family's relocation and transformation journey.

My Family's Relocation Chronology

Olivia and Arturo

The family relocation and transformation journey began in the late sixties. My youngest sister, Olivia, who married at age sixteen in 1961, left home the following year at age seventeen, and moved to an inner-city area in Brooklyn. To our surprise, and with much dismay, we witnessed our first family members take a risk and leave home. However, this was short-lived. In 1968, eight years later, Olivia and two of their children traveled by air while her husband and one child rode a bus across the country to Los Angeles, more than three thousand miles away. They left the family fold and we were all amazed by their bold but exciting move. This was the launching of the "Transformation and Relocation Journey" for our family.

My Mother, Maya

Four years later, in 1972, my mother who we called "Mother" was the next relative to leave New York City. She was age fifty-eight at this time. We were all grown and simultaneously independent so there was no real reason for her to stay in New York. Her only obstacle was her concern for her youngest son, William. My brother had breached one of the most important core values that must be established in any successful relationship. He breached the emotion of *"trust."*

During this time in my mother's life, we had all left home except William. Since he had dropped out of college, his days were pretty idle as he did not have a job. Of course, my mother was very concerned about his whereabouts during the day, especially since she suspected that he was using drugs. The last straw regarding William's behavior was when my mother returned home from work and discovered that her son, like a thief in the night, had betrayed her. He had stolen the huge refrigerator out of our kitchen, maneuvered it through various rooms to the front door, carried it down the stairs in broad daylight, and desperately sold it for drugs. I can only envision the look on my mother's face when she saw a gaping hole where her refrigerator once stood. Not only was Mother heartbroken and felt violated, she had to figure out a quick way to purchase a new refrigerator on her limited income. Outside of her immediate family concerns, she was also in a long-term destructive and abusive relationship with a man she was dating. Over time, her dysfunctional personal relationship and William's addiction and addicted behavior heightened to the point where it was obviously affecting Maya's days and nights. Each week, we actually saw the stress written all over her face worsen. All of her children, as well as my father, were disturbed about her physical and mental health.

Although my parents were separated for many years, Daddy was always in our lives and knew Maya's character very well. Applying a well-thought out strategy leading to positive results was my father's way! In preparation for implementation of his strategy, he reached out to my sister and her husband on the West Coast to get permission for my mother to relocate. Daddy's tactic was to protect Maya from their son's self-destructive behavior, as well as her dysfunctional relationship with her boyfriend, by removing her from the environment. Daddy knew if Maya thought she was permanently departing from New York, being as family-oriented as she was, she would have protested as she would not be willing to leave her children and grandchildren. So, my father's covert mission for our mother was for her to visit with my sister Olivia and her family for just a few weeks at his expense. He said, "You need the rest." Since she had never experienced travelling by plane and had not seen her youngest daughter in four years, she reluctantly agreed. Maya then made arrangements with her employer, stating that she was going on vacation and would return in a few weeks. Daddy then proceeded to confidentially purchase a one-way ticket with the idea that California would eventually grow on her as well as save her life.

Years later, I heard my mother's side of the story. She shared with me her sad, but awakening experience of being duped by my father. Maya was specifically angry with my father as she felt she was hoodwinked into entering through a door of no return. For the first few months, she was hanging on by her eyelashes until she could hold on no more. As time passed, her only hope was that she would eventually return to New York. After wallowing for a few months in uncontrollable tears, nostalgia, and resentment towards my father, my mother subsequently *moved out of her own way*. Maya began to accept the reality of her situation.

Being as independent as she has been for most of her adult life, this segment of her life was extremely challenging. She had no job, no money, and lived dependently under the roof of my sister Olivia and her husband, Arturo, and their three young children. This was tough for a number of reasons: mother, daughter, son-in-law, and grandchildren living in the same house is a challenge in its own right. To make matters even more stressful, my sister's husband is from Puerto Rico, and maintained a different culture from what my mother was accustomed. This also added to Maya's dilemma. Her unfamiliarity with these new standards and expectations was challenging as she had no choice at this time but to resort to dependency as well as control.

Maya eventually, courageously, shifted her mindset from resentment to optimism. With this new perspective of acceptance, my mother began to realize that the West Coast was beginning to agree with her. She ultimately became gainfully employed, found her own apartment, nurtured friendships, and fell in love with the landscape of the beautiful white-capped mountains, year-around sunny climate, and the peace and tranquility of a new life. The only downside was that she was on the West Coast and her other four children were on the East Coast.

However, Maya grew to love the West Coast so much that she requested that she live out her life there, including her burial. In the end, due to a cancer-related illness that ultimately took her life, Maya never returned to the City of New York to live again. You see, thirty years before, although initially uncomfortable, my mother learned to *moved out of her own way* to create a life worth living.

As expressed earlier, my father knew Maya's character very well. I learned over time that Daddy was responsible for three significant transformations in my mother's life. Two of these transformations had a positive impact, while, unfortunately, one was quite negative. The first positive transformation was Maya's marriage to Daddy in 1938 at the age of twenty-four. She was very much in love with my father and, for the first time in her life, free from the emotional and psychological chains of her mother's demands.

The second transformation unfortunately was negative. This happened during their traumatic separation in 1948 when my father's sexual orientation was revealed. Finally, Maya's relocation to California was the third transformation which resulted in a positive outcome. With the exception of the smog, California turned out to be very good for my mother. It was totally different from the hustle and bustle of life that she experienced in New York. It gave her a chance to shed the years of duress and anxiety that had become her life in the big city. In retrospect, I believe my father knew what he was doing in each instance.

My Daughter, Myishia

My daughter, Myishia was the third family member to leave New York. In August 1985, at age twenty-five and living independently, she was struggling with many esteem issues regarding her identity as a same-gender loving woman. Under my influence, guidance and support, Myishia relocated to Altadena, California, an upscale artist community, to live with my mother, her grandmother. This relationship didn't last very long, as Myishia's youth and adventuresome spirit caused her to feel smothered, restricted, and hypocritical in her new and confined environment. Myishia has always been very intelligent, creative, and free-spirited. She therefore desired her independence and pursued it. She eventually moved out and onward toward autonomy, independence, and self-determination to free herself to simply feel whole. Myishia searched for this independence for close to three decades and finally found it in 2010.

My Nieces, Marie and Lillian

In 1992, my brother Malvane's youngest daughter, Marie, was the next family member to spread her wings and leave the east coast. This was a courageous move for her as she was also leaving most of her family, including her parents, two sisters, and stepfather. Nonetheless, her eyes were set on migrating to the "New South". As a single mom at the time, Marie's purpose was to move from the busy and sometimes hazardous streets of New York City to a safer and more secure environment for her two young boys, ages five and seven. During the eighties and nineties, the streets of New York were becoming more and more crime-oriented and she maintained the desire to gracefully exit before her boys became teenagers.

One summer day, after due diligence in identifying their new living space, she and her best childhood friend, Diane, took the risk and relocated to Atlanta, Georgia. As several months passed, they raved so much about their new southern environment, with its predictably warm weather and progressive culture, others were influenced to follow. A year later, Marie's older sister, Lillian, followed her sister and took the path to Atlanta to begin a new life in the south. Marie and Lillian became the family pioneers who planted the seed for the family's migration to the "New South".

My Brother, Malvane

In 1995, three years after his daughters left New York, it was my brother's turn to transform his life. A diehard New Yorker, Malvane never wanted to leave the city he loved and established profound memories. He is a gregarious person who had many childhood friends who were still intimately involved in his life. He desired to hold on to the nurtured relationships he developed over the years with friends who graduated with him from high school, travelled with him in the U.S. and to other countries, shared social gatherings together, and in some instances, were employed in the same workplace.

At age fifty-four, he apparently became stuck. While in the prime of his life, Malvane was heading down a destructive path. We knew it and he knew it. For over a decade, we observed his hardships as well as dysfunctional behavior. Therefore, Roland and I intervened and gave him whatever support we could. Again, in 1995, we made arrangements with my mother, requesting her permission for Malvane to live with her, to which she agreed. This was ten years after my daughter left New York for California.

Malvane had always stood fast in his position that he really dislikes change. Considering his emotional attachment to the "Big Apple" and his inherent resistance to change, leaving New York City was not an easy process for him. In fact, the transition of saying good bye was very difficult for him. Nonetheless, Malvane ultimately relocated to California to save himself and simultaneously help our aging mom.

While there, he renewed his mindset from being stuck and resisting change to relaxing his position through acceptance of a new journey, a new environment, and a new chapter in his life. He became a constant companion to our mother, gained new experiences and insight into appreciating the West Coast culture, created a host of new friends, and also enhanced his education. However, like his mother, Malvane always expected to return to his roots on the east coast, and live the life to which he was accustomed. Yet he too ultimately moved out of his own way. He was now the sixth family member to leave home by *moving out of his own way.*

Roland and I

January 1998 was the year that I officially retired. My precious time belonged to no one except me. I loved this phase of my life! I was keenly aware that I now had a blank canvas in front of me to create whatever I wanted. The freedom was so exhilarating!

In 1991, in preparation for this day, I started my own consulting enterprise primarily to focus on full time after retirement, but for now I placed it on a back burner. I was emotionally and physically exhausted. I officially started working at age fourteen, married at age nineteen, raised two children, earned my GED and went through an emotionally draining divorce. While working full time, I also earned my undergraduate as well as two advanced degrees. However, my hard work, focus, and ability to actualize a vision to create my own business paid off. After fourteen years in high-level challenging executive positions, at age fifty-five, I finally retired with pride in my accomplishments, but exhausted.

For the first time in years, I was now able to dream and remember what I dreamt! I could literally open my eyes when I wanted to, plan my day as I sought fit, and choose to stay up as long as I desired without thoughts of physical retribution. For the first time in my life, it was my time to do absolutely nothing. Roland was still gainfully employed and left the house daily at 6:30 A.M. My time was my own! Outside of dinner preparation and housekeeping chores, there were no demands, no one to nurture, and no major commitments. For seven months, it was a great sabbatical for me. I loved it!

Infamously, the nineties were the initial decade of employee downsizing, reorganization, mergers and acquisitions, and what a buzz word, "Reengineering" became. For the first time in decades, there was a traumatic shift in loyalty between managers and staff. Prior to 1990, American organizations were considered loyal to their employees in the workplace. Managers, professionals, and staff usually remained in their organizations until retirement. This shift in workplace dynamics was the beginning of a new day for many corporate leaders, managers, and employees who were still in the workplace.

At the time, Roland was an executive in a well-known health care industry as Director of Medicaid Operations. That

Friday, late afternoon, he arrived home earlier than usual. He immediately shared the news with me that he was suddenly and unexpectedly dismissed from his position of four years. How could this be? There were no performance issues that I knew of and his sales ratings were great! In response to my many questions, I was told that his current manager had been let go the night before due to this reorganization or "Reengineering" process. Roland was as surprised as I was to hear of this "Reengineering" process that cost him his job. However, this news was the beginning of a new era in both of our lives.

After the initial shock, my bitter tears and the emotional conversation following this news, we put God's plan into action. The reality was that we were both now unemployed; we therefore had to move quickly. In my thinking, finding new employment might be a hurdle, but in no way is it an obstacle to stepping into the "Relocation and Transformation" journey that I had already envisioned for us. I felt in my spirit that we had to *move out of our own way* and transform our lives in order to follow God's plan. I knew in that moment that I had to continue my quest to create a life worth living.

With our commitment to move forward, we clearly rationalized that there was no major reason for either of us to remain connected to the Big Apple, despite our family ties in New York. Seldom did we see our families; mostly just holidays. I rarely spent time with my son and daughter-in-law who were caught up in their busy professional lives as well as in their religious obligations as Jehovah Witnesses. Roland also had family in New York, but his major bonds were with his mother and grandmother who had passed away a few years earlier. Like me, Roland was leaving the only place he ever lived.

During that unforgettable weekend, it took hours of influencing Roland that in order to save ourselves from losing everything we created together, relocating was the right decision. We had many assets, more liabilities, a savings plan, but no projected income. Even though Roland was marketable and more than likely will be re-employed in the City of New York, there was no guarantee of this probability. I personally felt that the odds were against us. Nonetheless, God was guiding us to a new life.

At that time in our discussion, we were considering Charlotte, North Carolina, but we were still not sure how to proceed. We both were planning to say good-bye to our siblings, aunts, uncles, nieces, nephews, and cousins. We also knew that Roland's siblings will not take this transition well. This was a frightening and risky time for both of us. I was uncertain how it would end, despite my belief that God was in control.

Fortunately, we had relatives in Atlanta, Georgia. Over the years, we had visited my nieces, Marie and Lillian, in the New South. Whenever we visited, they regularly made attempts to persuade us to relocate to Atlanta. Marie was single when she left New York in the early nineties, but now she was married to Douglas, her debonair new husband. We often stayed with the young couple in their beautiful home, visiting landmarks with them and learning about places of interest. We were both taken with the quality of life, the temperate weather, and the lush beauty of the area. Each time we visited, Roland and I came to appreciate life in the New South and seriously gave thought to relocating. It wasn't long before we learned that purchasing a house in Georgia was half the asking price in New York. This became the clincher. Prior to our final move, we again visited Atlanta, found our dream home, processed a mortgage, and set our wheels in motion.

Once back in New York, we immediately initiated our relocation strategy by selling assets, including the sale of our summer home in upstate New York, and finally began the arduous task of packing. This was in late August 1998, and it was then that we shared the news of our pending relocation with family and friends. Many people were in shock because of our sense of urgency and what seemed to them to be a sudden decision. They thought we were running away from something mysterious. To the contrary, we were really running toward God's blessing…a new life!

Three months later, on November 7th, 1998, we moved into our new home, two blocks from where my niece, Marie, lived with her husband Douglas and their blended family of three children. We quickly became accustomed to our lives in the suburbs of Atlanta.

Three months after we arrived, God's Divine Intervention was at work again. Roland gained employment at an Atlanta-based health care organization maintaining a high-level position and compensation package comparable to his job in New York. This allowed me to continue living my dream of retiring for a full year. I happily set about using the time redesigning our new home.

During this period of change and renewal, I began looking for spiritual fulfillment. For two years, I sporadically attended about five different churches. I eventually found and ultimately joined the church I currently attend, Victory for the World Church located in Stone Mountain, under the leadership of Rev. Dr. Kenneth L. Samuel, Pastor. Again, I feel that God was ordering my steps.

When I first joined in 2002, Victory for the World was considered a mega-church holding approximately seven thousand members. However, over time, that number significantly decreased. Dr. Samuel's vision was to follow the teachings of Jesus Christ to include all people regardless of race, class, gender, or sexual orientation. This vision implementation was the impetus for the attrition in membership. Regardless, Dr. Samuel passionately chose to educate his current members on the importance of embracing all people, regardless of their differences. He therefore began to orchestrate his vision for an all-inclusive church under the denomination of the United Church of Christ; consequently, over a five-year period, we lost about three thousand members. Nonetheless, Dr. Samuel, an anointed man, never faltered in attaining his vision. To this date, because of his anointed wisdom, tenacity, thought-provoking sermons, amazing choir, and all-inclusive membership, both same-gender loving persons and heterosexuals, I am proud to still be a member. Roland and I are at peace, spiritually fulfilled, and grateful that we both followed Jesus when he said *"Do not judge lest you be judged. For in the way you judge, you will be judged; and your standard of measure, it will be measured to you." – Matthew 7:1-2*

During the next ten years, Roland and I became extremely close with our two nieces, Marie and Lillian. We also established, nurtured, and enjoyed our relationship with Marie's husband, Douglas, their three boys, Nashaun, Christopher, and Douglas, Jr. By now, they were also proud parents of their baby daughter, Isabel.

Today, we are grateful they were in our lives since my children and siblings were not yet with us. I believe we also filled a void in their lives as my nieces parents were still in New York and Douglas's family were in Alabama. This harmonious decade of quality time together was all about feeling valued, supported, and unconditionally loved. We did just about everything together including enjoying home cooked family dinners, dining in neighborhood restaurants, emotionally supporting each other as needed, family movie nights, and appreciating the unconditional love we had for each other. Since they also attended Victory, we also prayed together. It was certainly a life worth living as we relished in every minute of it.

Olivia and Arturo
Their Second Relocation

To everyone's surprise, in August 2003, thirty-five years after relocating to the West Coast from New York City, my sister and brother-in-law, Olivia and Arturo, decided to join our "Circle of Love" here in Atlanta. This shocking news caused an emotional reaction by every family member because it was beyond our wildest dreams; however, we were all very pleased with their decision. They once again chose to *move out of their own way* and physically and spiritually transitioned themselves to the unknown cities of the south.

Unfortunately, and unexpectedly, a few years prior to this decision, they buried their oldest son, Arturo, Jr. due to complications during an illness. He was only thirty-seven old. The pain his parents, siblings, and other family members experienced in the loss of my nephew, my sister's first-born son will always be remembered. Her husband, Arturo, was also obviously just as grief-stricken.

Nonetheless, they eventually decided to leave the West Coast. After raising three children, creating and retiring from professional careers, they were now ready to pursue the "Relocation and Transformation" journey that had become our family's bond. In doing so, they courageously and emotionally separated from their mothers, children, friends, and distant family members. Because family fundamentally needs family, a few years later, they were followed by their granddaughter, Alexandria and later, their daughter, Charrise.

Malvane – His Second Relocation

Five years after we relocated to Atlanta, in December 2003, as previously mentioned, my mother transitioned to be with her Maker. We were all there to send her off. Once our mother was no longer with us in the flesh, my brother, Malvane, now had the opportunity to leave California. Again, this was a difficult process. Not only was he still for mourning the loss of our mother, he also was immediately displaced from the apartment he and our mother resided in and enjoyed together for eight years as mother and son. Malvane also had many friends he developed over the years, as well as a West Coast memory bank filled with fond recollections. Yet, he acutely felt the void of his absent family. His mother was gone and his sister, Olivia and family, had also left the sunny state of California.

For the second time, Roland and I again planted a seed for Malvane to think about... relocating to Georgia. Due to his loneliness, he accepted. It was encouraging to know that he would be joining his retired siblings in Atlanta and, more importantly, he would be reestablishing a relationship with his daughters and grandchildren whom he not seen for many years.

In 2004, Malvane moved in with Roland and I until he was able to acclimate himself to a new culture, new environment, and new life. During this time, he became employed, adapted to his situation in living with his sister and brother-in-law, reconnected with his daughters and grandchildren, and learned the culture of the New South. During the five years Malvane resided with us, we bonded as adult siblings and learned to appreciate the "Circle of Love" that never ends. Today he still talks about the blessing this relocation and transformation journey has been for him.

My Son, J.R. and Madeline

Unexpectedly, in 2005, my son, J.R., and daughter-in-law were next in making a conscious choice to transform their lives outside of New York City. I was pleasantly surprised when they made the decision to reposition themselves. Although my son loved New York, like his Uncle Malvane, he never thought he would ever leave. Those thoughts would change dramatically in 2001.

J.R. and his wife personally experienced and witnessed the tragedy in New York City on September 11, 2001 and were eyewitnesses to the attacks by Al-Qaeda on the World Trade Center. While his decision to leave New York City was precipitated by September 11, today J.R. has no regrets. However, the emotional and psychological scars of that tragic day referred to as "9/11" will remain with him forever. Subsequently, under the egis of the "Circle of Love", they too joined us in our quest to fulfill our dream to complete the relocation of family to the New South. Unfortunately, their union dissolved since then and J.R. now resides with Roland and me.

Myishia – Her Second Relocation

Twenty-one tumultuous years later, Myishia made her way to Atlanta from the West Coast. For the first time in two decades Myishia and I were finally together as mother and daughter, living under the same roof. The year was 2005. However, again, this arrangement didn't last long. Myishia's relocation at that time only lasted nine months. Over the next decade, she continued on her a turbulent search to solidify her identity. She explored Greensboro, North Carolina for nine months, Wilmington, Delaware for twenty-four months, and Somerset, New Jersey for forty-eight months.

Myishia was always known as a free spirit with an adventurous soul. As she matured and began to reflect upon her need for family, Myishia finally centered herself and made some well thought-out decisions. Her steadfast and tenacious pursuit to *move out of her own way* and to find a place of peace and balance ultimately came to pass. Eventually, Myishia came full circle with her life, solidified her identity as a same-gender loving woman, found love, and returned to Atlanta in 2014 where she currently resides with her partner.

Roberta and Levertis

Do you remember, my sister Roberta? It was she and I who, thirty years prior, created the dream of being together in our golden years and uniting the family in one location. When Roberta and Levertis finally retired, they sold their first home, and moved into their second home in upstate New York in the Poconos. We all loved the Poconos' family gatherings, but most of us now lived in the "Bible Belt" in the State of Georgia.

When this plan didn't work out for them, they enthusiastically began the process of entering into the "Relocation and Transformation" journey. Finally, in 2006, my older sister, Roberta, and her husband Levertis, followed the family vision and moved to Atlanta. We were ecstatic that this had come to pass! The sisters were back together again dreaming, creating and planning, just as we did nearly three decades ago.

It is very rewarding for both of us to once again see our dreams become a reality. To add to their contentment, in 2009, three years later, their daughter, Elizabeth, her husband, Edward, and their two girls followed. What a life worth living!

Elizabeth and Edward

Elizabeth and her husband, Edward, a rising high-level executive in the healthcare industry were repositioned a number of times during their marriage due to his career opportunities. One of these significant and life changing moves included Edward's wish to relocate to his birthplace and his large family in Chicago. This move was actualized and lasted for about five years.

Over the course of twelve years, the birth of two daughters, and six different households, Elizabeth also missed her biological family. She eventually influenced Edward to meet her emotional needs and the needs of their children by relocating to Georgia to be near her parents and her Atlanta family.

In 2009, three years after her parents relocated to Georgia, my sister's daughter, Elizabeth and her family finally reached a decision to relocate for the seventh and final time. By announcing their decision to move to Atlanta, the "Circle of Love" is almost complete. We are still waiting for her twin brother, Levertis, Jr. to join us. We pray it will be real soon.

Irma and Thomas

Surprisingly, the next family to join us in Atlanta was a life-long friend, Irma, who is more like a sister than a friend. Irma has been in my life since we were six years old when we met in the first-grade in Catholic school. She is actually the ex-wife of my brother, Malvane, and the mother of my three nieces, Marie, Lillian, and Michelle.

Actually, considering Irma and Thomas are the last family members to join our "Relocation and Transformation" journey, Irma was the first person to introduce me to Atlanta, Georgia. One balmy spring evening while living in New York, Irma and Lewis were planning to visit their daughters and grandchildren in Georgia. For some reason, a few hours before they were leaving, Irma invited me to join them on this fourteen-hour road trip. I had never been that far south before and was a bit curious. I knew it was going to be a long drive, but I actually had no plans for the weekend. This was also the year that I had retired. They said they were returning on Monday which was fine with me. . Contrary to my usual distain for making spontaneous decisions and after discussing this trip with Roland, I accepted. However, it was God's voice that guided me to accept the invitation. My response was so unusual for me. Today I realize that this was God's divine intervention.

Ironically, while it was her daughter Marie who was the impetus for this family transition, Irma, her husband, Thomas, their daughter, Michelle, and her four children finally joined our family in the Bible Belt in 2011. They ultimately moved out of their own way to take this leap toward further happiness and contentment. We were now all here in Georgia creating a "Circle of Love".

My Surrogate Family: Charlene and Anthony

My surrogate family of four is also from our northern roots. I've known Charlene since she was fourteen and I mentored her as a young woman. She lived in the next building from mine in Co-op City in the Bronx. Due to our close proximity, I also knew her mother, father, and brother. I didn't know her sister as well because she lived in another state.

Our relationship really blossomed while I was dating Roland, my current husband. Charlene worked in a restaurant part-time where Roland and I frequently visited. Straight out of college, I was influential in helping her to seek a permanent employment position. She subsequently became successfully employed for many years in the same organization where I was working.

When Charlene married in 1998, she and her husband, Anthony, along with their two-year old son, followed the trend and in 1999 relocated to Atlanta. Four years later, they were blessed to have a second son.

Unfortunately, Charlene lost her mother to cancer in 2006. Subsequently, Roland and I were privileged to become surrogate grandparents to her two sons. Her dad also lived in Atlanta with his new wife. What a blessing they have been to us, and our biological family. Charlene and her family, including her dad and stepmother, have been in our lives ever since.

The "Circle of Love" Family Day

In honor of our parents, in 2003, Roland and I established a "Circle of Love" Family Day where we meet on the last Saturday of each month in alternate homes. This "Circle of Love" monthly celebration is considered to be a mandatory social function with the goal of appreciating our family ties. There are now twenty-seven family members who participate. Each family member contributes to the dinner menu whatever is requested by the host and hostess. It turns out to be quite a feast.

On Family Day, everyone shows up on time for prayer before dinner and fellowship afterwards. Immediately after prayer, one of us tells a light story about a parent who has deceased. We believe in the African proverb, "As long as we speak their name, they still live in our hearts." In this way, we don't lose the purpose behind creating "The Circle of Love" Family Day.

Often, and not surprisingly, challenges can arise when trying to consistently get together for occasions such as this. But we make it a joyous occasion and keep things grounded and meaningful by discussing our values, sharing family history, addressing present challenges and remembering past challenges. As always, we talk about how we can be supportive of each other. Today, after thirteen years of launching this monthly event of honoring our parents and ancestors as a family unit, we individually and collectively honor our time together as a serious event. In other words, we do everything we can to be in attendance to maintain our parents' legacy.

With the exception of three single and independent nephews, and one family man living in California with his daughter and wife, we are almost one full circle of love. We are close to being one unified family that is filled with love and many stories of our past. We now live together in the southern hemisphere of the United States, no more than twenty miles apart from each other, without an ounce of bitterness or regret. Because of the size and forces at work in our family to finally accept each other for who we are, we've gone through the dynamic stages of "Forming", "Storming", "Norming", and "Performing". Each time a new family or family member joins our "Circle of Love", we inevitably return to the "Forming" stage.

The "Forming" stage is when we are relatively new to the circle and behave in such a way that nurtures the intact relationships through respectful and non-invasive behavior. In this stage, we are acclimating ourselves to the family norms through observance as well as active participation. Eventually, perhaps a few months of gathering as a group, the testing of the group parameters precipitates the "Storming Stage".

In the "Storming" stage, we unconsciously begin to challenge each other through debate, discussion, or encounters to see how far we can go before there is a pushback. This stage could also be labeled "infighting". Although we unconditionally love each other, during the "Storming" stage, which also can go on for a few weeks or months, we are basically being prepared for the next stage, the "Norming" stage.

During the "Norming" stage, the element of time allows us to get to know each other's strengths and weaknesses, likes and dislikes, and differences in personality types. Although we, at some point in our family relationships, may have had some disdain for another family member, and even gossiped about each other, in the end we forgive and accept each other with all of our differences. It takes a little time to get through this stage before we can consider ourselves to be at the last stage, called the "Performing" stage.

This fourth stage is the culminating stage where we have surpassed the niceties and infighting. At this stage, we move toward acceptance of diverse personalities, behaviors, and the unique gifts that God has given each of us. Subsequently, as a family unit, we slowly transition through each process where we finally attest to our unconditional love for each other. This stage is called the "High Performing" stage where most families or teams want to be. At this stage, we come full circle by consistently exemplifying our genuine respect for each other in the "Circle of Love". We are now on one accord and ultimately productive.

Considering a history of a dysfunctional family life while growing up, our parents would have been proud of each of us for *moving out of our own way* and honoring the sanctity of family. What a blessing to know we are developing this family legacy! What a life worth living!

My Self-Worth Today

Looking back on my life, I know I was part of a dysfunctional family. Perhaps it would have been a different outcome in my developmental years if my dad were around more often. Perhaps it would have been different if I had not been the middle child. Perhaps if I had heard more messages of inspiration while growing up as a child or young adult, my self-esteem would have been higher. Some parents are very encouraging with consistent affirming words of support; some parents are unconsciously discouraging with on-going negative words or put downs; some parents are void of doing either! During my childhood, an example of "not doing either" was simply my mother's way.

During my spiritual awakening, I learned a few things. I learned that my existence was filled with many thought-provoking life experiences, the good and the bad. Becoming a mother at a young age, enduring an abusive first marriage, surviving a life-threatening illness, and managing a painful divorce did not deter me from moving out of my own way to remarry and to create a life worth living.

God sent to me my soul mate with whom I share a blessed married life today. I also have reestablished a close and loving relationship with both of my formally estranged children, one who lives with me, and one who now lives nearby. Because Roland and I are equally yoked, we continue to focus on God first, then on family, faith and fulfillment and have formed a "Circle of Love", specifically on "Family Day" to maintain a life worth living.

Today, instead of allowing negative experiences to become obstacles in my life, I choose to capitalize on them. With God's guidance and the divine intervention of my guardian angels, I have moved out of my own way to overcome these setbacks. When we first moved to Georgia, there were only eight of us. Now there are twenty-seven. As it was when we were younger and living in New York, our holidays are still important to us today. On many occasions, I pause, count my blessings, and as needed, *move out of my own way*, to ensure that we continue to nurture our relationships in the interest of maintaining this life that is worth living.

The Power of Now

As Eckhart Tolle, author of "The Power of Now" writes, "People don't realize that NOW is all there is; there is no past or future except as memory or anticipation in your own mind." I did not fully understand the "Power of Now" and the impact nineteen years of marriage had on the balance of my life or that of my children until "Now". However, today, I do know the importance of being in the "Now". I currently live each day with this thought in mind, as I consciously know two things:

1. God is in total control of my destiny.
                    and
2. Tomorrow is not promised.

    In closing, God is my guiding light in creating and maintaining a life worth living. My level of inner peace comes from this guiding light.   Today we are living in a world that is filled with change and uncertainty. Therefore, inner peace is needed! I pray that some of my shared experiences, testimonies, as well as my mindset will also help you to look within, move out of your own way, and create a life worth living.   As said earlier, only God knows how the story will end.

> We are not permitted to choose the frame of our destiny. But what we put into it is ours.
>
> Dag Hammarskjoid

May God continue to bless you, lead you, and fill you with His Holy spirit.

The Hysmith Group

hysmithgroup.com

www.ingramcontent.com/pod-product-compliance
Lightning Source LLC
Chambersburg PA
CBHW060817190426
43197CB00038B/1830